RICHARD CLUBLEY was born by island encounter was with the tl Withernsea beach at very low tide. was either covered by the sea or easily walkable to from the bottom of the beach, so hardly an island. Nevertheless, it caused a stir in the blood of local under tens when it appeared, around the time of full and new moons, and perhaps this is what sparked Richard's life-long fascination with islands.

There was also Bull Sand Fort in the Humber estuary and then Arran on a family holiday. The islands in North Bay Lido, Scarborough also made quite an impression when, unable to swim, he got marooned on one and had to be rescued by the tall lifeguard who hardly got his trunks wet in the process.

Howsoever it came about, Richard caught the incurable island fever or nesomania. In 2017, Richard, Bev and Dog moved to live in Orkney, having bought a plot of land overlooking Scapa Flow and built a house.

As a biology teacher in London and Sheffield, Richard took groups of children to explore Mull, Iona and the uninhabited islands of Staffa and Lunga off the west coast of Scotland and many of them caught the bug too. He is now a regular contributor to Scottish Islands Explorer and www.Orkney.com. Over the course of his adult life, he has explored around 90 (so far) of the Scottish islands. This is his third book about them.

LIZ THOMSON trained as a teacher before taking up her brush and pencils and graduated from Sheffield School of Art in 1979. Her work is regularly exhibited both locally – in Sheffield, where she still lives and nationally. Liz won a major prize for landscape in the 2001 Laing competition and was a regional finalist in the 2005 competition for Channel 5. Her work hangs in private collections in the USA, Holland Austria and France, as well as here in the UK.

# Orkney

## *A Special Way of Life*

RICHARD CLUBLEY
with illustrations by LIZ THOMSON

**Luath** Press Limited
EDINBURGH
www.luath.co.uk

The chapters in Part One appeared on www.Orkney.com between 2016 and 2019. Part Two stories were previously published in *Living Orkney* magazine.

First published 2021

Reprinted 2021

ISBN: 978-1-913025-44-1

The paper used in this book is recyclable. It is made from low chlorine pulps produced in a low energy, low emission manner from renewable forests.

Printed and bound by Severn, Gloucester

Typeset in 10.5 point Sabon by Lapiz

All photographs by Richard Clubley unless otherwise indicated. Illustrations and maps by Liz Thomson

Pair of eider ducks – copied by permission of Tim Wootton.

*To the memories of my father and mother,
Raymond and Barbara, and to the hope of a bright
future for their great grandson – Rémy – born 100 years
later. Four generations, 50 times over, take us back to
when the first farmers lived at the Neolithic village
of Skara Brae, Orkney. It seems a blink of an eye to
that earlier life.*

# Contents

PART TWO: The Orkney Way of Life on the Outer Islands

PART THREE: Living by the Sea

PART FOUR: Conclusions, Looking Back and
            Looking Forward

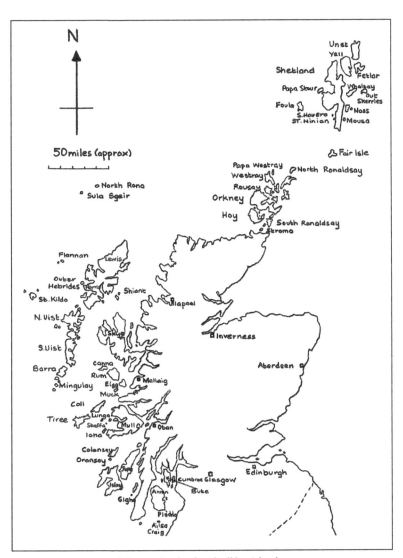

Map 1 – Scotland with all her islands.

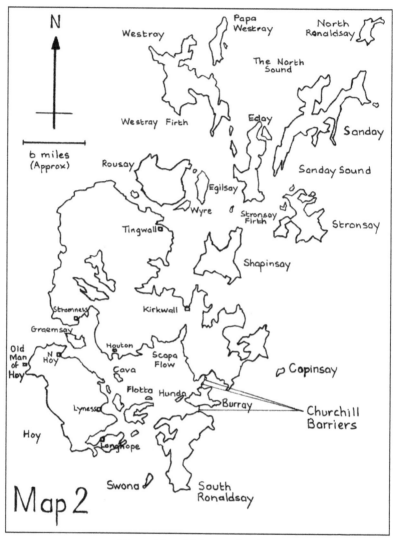

Map 2 – Map of Orkney archipelago.

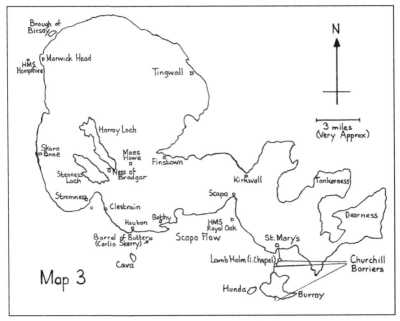

Map 3 – Map of Orkney Mainland.

# Acknowledgements

A big thank you to everyone who has helped, in any way, with this book.

Thanks to Gavin MacDougall and everyone at Luath for sound advice and guidance.

Thanks to John Humphries, and more recently Melissa Silver, at *Scottish Islands Explorer* magazine, Andrew Learmonth at www.Orkney.com, John Ross Scott and Cheryl Chapman at *Living Orkney* for their support and encouragement and for publishing some of the stories in the run up to this book.

Thanks to everyone who has looked at the final manuscript but the responsibility for any errors or omissions is entirely mine. The pace of change, especially in communications and renewable energy is so great that some of my statements are out of date as soon as I write them but I hope the sentiments and principles still hold good.

A big thank you must go to the people of Orkney for making Bev, Dog and me so welcome since we moved here from Derbyshire in 2017. As they were for the first Orkney Book (*Orkney: A Special Place*), they have continued to be open and honest about their islands and provide many of the stories for this one.

Thanks to Bob Budge and B&L Builders for our lovely warm house. Bob is sadly missed.

Another big thank you to Liz Thomson for more of her super drawings. Her enthusiasm for both illustration and meeting the deadline is highly valued. Also thanks to Tim Wootton for permission to copy his paintings of owls and ducks, and Barry Johnston for use of his lifeboat photograph.

Last but not least, much love and thanks to Bev for unwavering support and encouragement throughout. Especially thank you, Bev, for giving up your life south to live in Orkney. I know you worried you wouldn't have enough to do but I hope everyone was right when they said, 'Your problem will be fitting it all in.'

*Richard Clubley, 2021*

# Preface

ORKNEY IS NOT idyllic but I love life here, having wanted to move here for a very long time. I felt at home the second I drove off the ferry in September 2017 to begin this new way of life. There has not been a moment of doubt or a second thought since.

I have been very lucky. There are people who, having experienced a gale on their first weekend, catch the boat south again on Monday morning. Incomers come prepared for the first winter. Having heard so much about the weather in advance, they grit their teeth and bear it. Day length soon starts to increase again after Christmas so they breathe a sigh of relief and say, 'That wasn't so bad and it's almost over already.' Then the winter drags on for several more months and spring is a long time coming. When the glorious daffodils do, finally, arrive (daffodils *are* glorious all over Orkney), 'new islanders' forget they have to do it all over again after a few short months of summer.

Over the years, perhaps beginning with an influx of hippies in the 1960s and self-sufficiency folk during the 1970s, people have come here seeking the peaceful life they imagine and have read about. They believe that, magically, all their troubles will be washed away by the sea, or blown away by the fresh air but this is not necessarily the case. Later on in the book, I have included some writing by school students in Orkney. I visited schools in Kirkwall, Sanday, Stronsay and Hoy to hear what the youngsters had to say about their islands. Children and young adults do not mince words. Alex Gibson (17) of Kirkwall Grammar School has written very movingly and eloquently about what pain and trouble can be hidden behind the tourist façade in Orkney.

In spite of our wonderful reputation for renewable energy in the form of wind turbines and the development of wave and tidal power, there is real fuel poverty in some households. (Fuel poverty is defined as needing to spend more than 10 per cent of income on domestic heating.) The old croft houses are charming and contribute to the romantic notion of living on a Scottish island. 'Let's move to Orkney, buy an old croft house and do it up,' people say, only to find the house is cold and damp and they can't fit new windows because it is a listed building. Internal insulation might be possible but reduces the room sizes.

There are all the other things you might be familiar with too: council decisions and indecisions; road closures; hospital waiting lists; school budgets; crime (mercifully minor, most of the time); food bills and, yes, even some people you'll find yourself not getting on with. Add to that the cost of travel, ferry cancellations and plane delays, and you begin to get the picture.

You may by now be wondering why I bothered to write this book and why you are considering possibly buying and reading it. Be strong. Stay with me. There *is* a special way of life to be had in Orkney. In our first year, we had 16 sets of visitors from among our friends and family and they all went away stunned by what they had seen and experienced – even those who had thought we were crazy making the move. Jane arrived after just three weeks and, while the house was still littered with packing cases, she said, 'I totally get it now.'

# Introduction

WHAT DO WE mean by 'way of life'? How many different ways of life are there in Orkney?

Archaeologists tell us that when humans changed from being hunter/gatherers they found a new way of life in farming. It was a sudden transition, in archaeological terms, round about 5,000 ago. Neolithic people – farmers – arrived in Orkney and transformed the way of life of the resident hunter/gatherers. There does not seem to have been an armed conflict; rather, the hunters saw the new techniques, liked what they saw and thought they'd give it a go. It might have been the first significant change to the way of life in human history.

Hunter/gathering didn't end altogether – it never has. People have always recognised a source of food when they see one: brambles, mushrooms, fish and winkles are hunted and gathered in the 21st century.

The hunters must have seen something attractive in farming as it is actually more labour intensive than hunting and gathering. It is more difficult to take a day off when there are animals to be tended. On the other hand, one can put down roots. Farmers can have solid, permanent houses that don't need to be moved; they can have bigger families (more food can be produced to feed hungry mouths and some surplus can be stored); they can have dominion over their own territory more readily. They may have come into some conflict over this. The hunters may have seen the territory as theirs. The farmers laid claim to the land, we think, by building burial cairns and stone henges as a way of saying, 'Look, our ancestors are here – we own this – keep off' (maybe).

Everybody was a hunter/gatherer, there was no division of labour, except maybe some were hunters and some gatherers and childminders. The way of life was hunter/gathering though. Men and women lived by the fruits of the two endeavours. Once the land was cultivated and many of the trees cleared, hunting and gathering became difficult even if they had wanted to continue. The more people cleared the land and the more the population grew, the more land they needed. Pretty soon Orkney was one big farm – as it more or less is today. Hunter/gathering gave way to a new way of life.

We don't know when division of labour took off, maybe very early on in the transformation. Maybe stone axe-making, herding, ploughing, clothes-making, house-building, cooking and even trading became specialist occupations at the very beginning. Stone axe-making is highly skilled. Some would have more facility in it than others and would naturally lean towards it as a profession. Perhaps one worker in the corner house was delighted to be inside all day making axes, out of the rain. Maybe he/she enjoyed it, found it easy, therapeutic even and smugly enjoyed having his or her meals prepared and clothes made in return.

My daughter once complained to me she had been woken by Sunday morning church bells. I said I thought church bells had been a tradition for quite a long time and, anyway, I rather liked them. This set me to wondering whether church bells had been the first, unwelcome by some, environmental noise. They certainly predate internal combustion engines, electric devices, steam engines etc. What about stone axe-making? I thought. How long did one take to make? How long did they last? How many would have been needed? Was the 'workshop' deliberately placed at the edge of the village, and detached from it, to lessen the noise nuisance for the other villagers? Did people ever say, 'I wish Barney Rubble would give it a rest with his hammering and knapping, I've got a terrible headache and I want to sleep'?

So, is there only one 'way of life' in Orkney – farming? There are those who till the soil and herd the sheep. They are clearly the farmers. But what about the van and lorry drivers, the millers, the butchers, the retailers, the delivery people, the inspectors, the bank managers, the builders and repairers? Are they farmers too? Is their way of life in farming, albeit a small part of it? They all cooperate with the 'farmer' to get the food to the dinner plate. (And what about the potters making the plates, the manufacturers of washing up liquid, cutlery and dishwashers? Are they all subsisting because of a farming way of life?)

In the animal kingdom, it is easier to identify a few different ways of life. There are the carnivores, the herbivores and parasites. These, I think, can fairly be called different ways of life. The animals in question derive their livings by fundamentally different ways of operating in their environments. I'll stop now; maybe I'm making too much of this. Opticians, schoolteachers and wind turbine service engineers may take a dim view of me calling them all farmers.

I cannot think of Orkney without my mind going back to the men and women who built and lived in Skara Brae – a Stone Age village that has stood on the west coast of Orkney Mainland for over 5,000 years. The village was buried and preserved in sand after its abandonment about 4,000 years ago, until its rediscovery in 1850, when the sand blew away in a storm. No one is really sure if it was abandoned *because* a storm filled it with sand, or whether it was abandoned and then gradually filled with sand through neglect of the sweeping brushes.

Skara Brae was a farming community, one of the earliest in Orkney. Archaeologists think around 100 people lived in the ten buildings we can see today. There may have been more, long since eroded away by the sea and lost forever. There is a wide bay in front of the village today that was not there when Skara Brae was occupied. It is the result of erosion and rising sea levels (about 6m in the last 5,000 years).

The Skara Brae folk grew bere, an ancient form of barley, which they ground on quern-stones into flour. They probably made forms of bread, scones and bannocks just as we do today. There are only so many different ways you can cook flour over a fire, or hot stones, after all.

They kept sheep and pigs, caught fish, collected shellfish and birds' eggs. There were nuts and berries in their season. They herded cattle for meat and dairy produce. They had fleeces, hides and furs. They had a very good diet available to them (although there is some evidence that not everyone got an equal share). They were almost as big in stature as we are today.

The houses were sizeable – perhaps half the size of a modest, modern two-bed semi. Each was a single room for open-plan living but cosy for an extended family. They had thick, well-built walls, pitched and possibly thatched roofs. There is evidence of stone roofs at Ness of Brodgar – another Neolithic site in Orkney – but mostly it was probably thatch, hide or turf, or a combination. Being organic materials, no trace has survived to tell the tale. There would have been a central hearth for burning wood and peat and a low doorway with a screen leading to a sheltered passage that ensured protection from the elements (which, as we know, can be pretty elemental in Orkney). The villagers would have been snug indoors, and happy, provided they were content with conversations, story-telling, music, games and whatever work they could get on with in the low light. One of the houses is detached and may have been a workshop (possibly for stone axe-making).

I wonder how much the Orcadian way of life has changed. The islands are still predominantly farmland. The major industry today is farming. Tourism comes second but even that may not be new. We know that, 5,000 years ago, some of the stone for tools and even some finished pieces were brought in from elsewhere in the UK. This could have been by Orcadians travelling and bring back trade goods or even simple souvenirs. People from outside could have travelled here for the same reason.

Of course, there is a much greater division of labour now. Whereas the animal management, crop-growing, tool-making, building and sewing would all have been carried out by the group – much in the way crofting was practised until very recently – they are now much in the hands of specialists. Economies of scale allow some to specialise in meat production, milk production, distribution and provision of clothes. Whereas energy for heating and cooking was once collected and thrown on the hearth, now a lot comes down wires from generators elsewhere. A similar way of life is being supported though. In the official guide to the Ness of Brodgar, the Neolithic folk who built it are described as: intelligent, highly creative, sophisticated, spiritual, gregarious and competitive.

Way of life is difficult to define and perhaps we should just appreciate and enjoy ours without agonising too much about how to describe it or how it differs from other ways of life. Bev's mum, Edith, summed it up succinctly when, after several visits to Orkney, she declared, 'There seem to be a lot of farms round here.'

# Part One

---

CHAPTER ONE

# Orkney – A Special Place

---

THE MAN FROM www.Orkney.com promised faithfully to phone me on the Wednesday. He had heard I was writing about Orkney and wondered if I might like to contribute to www.Orkney.com. Late on Wednesday evening I received the following email from him:

> Hi Richard,
>
> This is going to sound like the most ridiculous excuse ever. The Royal Navy were carrying out a safe detonation of a WW2 torpedo that has been found on the seabed in Scapa Flow. It is thought to be one fired by Captain Gunther Prien, of U47, when he attacked and sank HMS *Royal Oak* lying at anchor in the Flow in 1939.
>
> I heard about it at the last minute so went out on the pilot boat to follow the story. I would have phoned you when it was all over but the first charge failed to destroy the weapon. It only dislodged from the seabed and floated to the surface. The Navy boys had to go back on shore for more explosives. They eventually detonated it at the surface so we got good pictures of the splash. Sorry.

The excuse was good, but not out of the ordinary for Orkney. Take, for instance, the time I chartered a local boat to take me and my camping gear to Cava:

> The pier has been washed away, I'm afraid, so you'll have to wade ashore. Can your dog swim?

Then again there was my local guide on an outer island who said:

> I'll have to pass you onto a colleague for the rest of the tour.
> The postmistress is away to Kirkwall for a tooth extraction,
> I have to serve behind the counter this morning so we can
> keep the post office open.

My town in Derbyshire has a population much the same as Orkney's but I have never been delayed by a torpedo or been roped into to sell stamps. I suppose these things could be described as frustrations but, for me, they are just part of what makes Orkney special.

I'm an outsider, of course. Had I lived in Orkney all my life I might have a different view, but I don't think so – the locals seem as fascinated by the islands as I am. There always seems to be 'news' in Orkney: ships arriving, festivals launching, weather happening, visitors calling and wildlife appearing. Everyone appears to love it. There are newspapers, magazines, radio stations, coffee mornings and blogs dedicated to keeping everyone informed, not to mention the island drums and smoke signals: 'Oh, aye, I heard that.'; 'Yes, I ken him.'; or 'No, you don't say?'

I have loved Scottish islands in general, and Orkney in particular, for much of my life but I still struggle to understand what makes them such special places. There is so much going on in Orkney it is bewildering at times. Before moving here I spent seven months here, in all seasons, and still managed to miss a lot. Even so, it was nice to open *The Orcadian*, see something advertised and think 'Great, I'll be here for that,' instead of, 'Oh dear, something else I'm going to miss.' I managed to catch the Ba', St Magnus Festival, the lunar eclipse at Ring of Brodgar (I'm sure I could have caught it at home, too, but there wouldn't have been people in flowery skirts, with bells tuned to the four elements and a winter gale).

It seems to me that, on an island, if you want something you have to provide it yourself. At home, if I want to go to the cinema, cathedral or airport I have to go out of town. Not so easy on an island, where a water crossing is involved, so Orkney has to be so much more self-sufficient.

Then there's the weather (different every minute but never bad, unless your clothes are inappropriate), whales, birds, seals, aurora, flowers, history and archaeology. There's power from the wind and waves and energy in the tides. There's vitality in the music and craft in the pottery. There's warmth in the whisky, style in the furniture and sparkle in the jewellery.

My wife, Bev, and I took the first step towards flitting to Orkney in 2016. We started by enquiring about a plot of land to buy on Mainland. An ex-Orkney lighthouse man I met described it as 'getting a shift'. I believe new folk are welcome in Orkney – especially if they contribute in some way to the community – I don't think I'll feel so much like a 'ferry louper' as a 'new islander'. Read on and see how the project progresses.

New Balfour Hospital, Kirkwall, opened in 2019.

## CHAPTER TWO

# Cantick Head Lighthouse

ISLAND EXPLORATION IS about many things. One requirement that comes up regularly is away-from-it-all-ness. 'We want to recharge our batteries, get away from work-a-day cares and woe, enjoy stunning views, peace and quiet, long walks and the sound of the sea,' people say. 'We'd like somewhere comfortable, after a day of weather, to dry out if necessary, cook good food, drink wine and relax with friends.' Look no further – Cantick Head has two beautifully decorated and well appointed, traditional lightkeepers' cottages.

Cantick Head is still a well maintained and nicely painted functional light tower. It marks the south-eastern tip of South Walls, attached to the southern tip of Hoy, Orkney. It looks out over the approaches to Scapa Flow. The sea is all around. On a clear night, other lights can be seen on Stroma, Swona, South Ronaldsay, Pentland Skerries and across the Pentland Firth at Dunnet Head and Duncansby Head. On some nights, the northern lights add to the show.

In our crowded British Isles, it requires effort to truly get away from it all. Orkney can be reached by a choice of sea and air routes. Then you must catch the small car ferry from Houton to Lyness on Hoy, which takes 30 minutes. The trick is to make the travelling part of the adventure, weaving between the deserted islands of Cava, Rysa Little and Fara. Flotta is interesting, with its oil terminal but – don't worry – it will be well out of sight long before you reach Cantick Head. Look out for Muckle House, now derelict, on Cava, where two English ladies lived after walking and pushing their belongings in a tea chest on wheels from Somerset. (Their story was told in detail in *Scotland's Islands – A Special Kind of Freedom*, Luath Press, 2017.)

From Lyness, it's a gentle 20-minute drive on a good road, then a few hundred yards of potholed track to your cottage. Depending on the season there might be kelp, ware or tangles (seaweed) strewn across the road from winter gales. But, just like the wind, the ware adds to the ambience.

You can fish from the rocks outside the lighthouse cottages – near enough for someone to carry a hot mug of tea down to sustain you in your effort to provide for the evening table in the traditional manner. But, if the weather isn't suitable for hunter/gathering, you have the whole of Hoy to explore: Martello towers, lifeboat museum, RNLI memorial, naval cemetery, Scapa Flow wartime museum (café and shop but check opening), the Dwarfie Stane, Betty Corrigall's grave and Rackwick Bay – then go to the pub.

Whatever you choose to do, don't forget to take a turn around the walled lawn last thing before retiring, see just how many other lighthouses you can count – and remind yourself of where you are and why you came.

Cantick Head lighthouse, South Walls – comfortable holiday lets.

CHAPTER THREE

# A Dream Come True

IT IS A dream come true. I know that's a cliché but it really is a dream come true. We bought half an acre of land on Mainland Orkney, overlooking Scapa Flow, and Bob Budge built us a house in which to live.

In the early days of my Orkney exploration, I would start to mourn the passing of the week, or fortnight, as it came to an end but in recent years I always had a few visits in the diary at any one time so, in leaving, I could look forward to returning.

My dream, though, has been to live here. When I put down my book and turn out the light each night, I like to fill those seven seconds (experts say it averages seven seconds) before I fall asleep, with a constructed fantasy: walking on a favourite beach; watching wildfowl through the reeds of a loch side or seeing the black/grey weather clouds rolling in over Ring of Brodgar.

Where to live in that fantasy has always been an issue. It being imaginary, there are no rules or limits. A grand old house by the sea, with policy woodland giving shelter from the storms perhaps, or maybe a stone bothy with walls three feet thick and a low roof for the wind to blow straight over. A period townhouse in Kirkwall might be nice, with spiral staircases, wooden banisters and an enclosed yard making a sun trap. Nipping out for coffee at a favourite café, or a browse in the bookshop, would be easy every day. Turning out in the evenings for theatre or cinema would be no hardship.

There were never any snags, setbacks or problems in the fantasy but, oh dear, when it became real, I had to start thinking about planning permission, costs, logistics – and what if the cat gets lost?

Each time I arrived in Orkney, after the long drive from south, and walked out on that favourite beach, I took in a deep, involuntary breath of contentment and elation. It was not done deliberately, it just happened. I guess it must be like how the hit of a powerful drug might feel. The late Roger Deakin, in *Waterlog*, his book about wild swimming in Britain, felt the endorphins in his blood when he swam in rivers and lakes – he called them 'endolphins'. I get a daily dose of endolphins since we moved.

Incidentally, Bev wanted to keep a couple of sheep on our new half-acre farm in Orkney. She thought it would be a neat, eco-friendly way of keeping the grass tidy. North Ronaldsay have been ruled out because of copper intolerance. Soay might be a bit wild. Any hints, advice or suggestions as to how we could do this, or why we shouldn't, would be gratefully received. I should stress these would be *pet* sheep, raised from caddy lambs, to provide wool and grass-cutting services only. They will live the life of Riley. I'm told I've to make a little house in the garden, to protect them from the worst of the winter gales. Don't be too surprised if you call round to see us and find them curled up in baskets in the kitchen – one either side of the Aga. In reality, a farmer neighbour has decreed we really don't have enough ground for two sheep. They need about half an acre each apparently. They'd be fine in summer but, in winter, would churn up the ground too much. It wouldn't be fair to keep just one. 'Don't bother with a goat either,' he said. 'If you get a goat you might as well fly a flag out front announcing yourselves as incomers.'

The builder gave me the number of a man who would seed a lawn for me at the new house but he didn't answer so I bought some seed and did it myself. The seed merchant said, 'Rake it first,' (and sold me a rake) but the ground was very hard (in August) and wide, so I didnae bother. The merchant also loaned me a spreader but it didnae spread so I broadcast it. I don't mean I told everyone about the faulty spreader, I mean I broadcast the seed – the old way – like Russell Crowe in *Robin Hood*.

Six weeks later, the lawn looked like the Giant's Causeway. The surface mud had dried and cracked into hexagonal patterns and the grass was only sprouting from the cracks. 'Give it time,' said the builder. 'It'll fill in.'

As summer turned to autumn, I ordered a mower and they said, 'It'll have tae come fae sooth, but dinna worry, they hae wan in the shop and they'll put it on the boat.'

They phoned to say the mower had arrived but our shed was still in sections on the drive, held down against the gales by a ton of breeze blocks borrowed from a neighbouring farm. I asked the lady if I could keep it in the conservatory for a bit. She said no so I asked the shop to hang on to the mower and they said, 'Nae bother.'

The shed went up and I called for the mower but they said, 'We sold it to someone else, but dinna worry we'll order another.' Weeks passed, the grass grew taller and the mower arrived so I cut the grass.

Autumn turned to winter and the paths became icy. The shop said, 'We've only two bags of salt left and they're saved for a customer.' I asked if they would do with the salt what they had done with my mower so they sold the salt to me.

The mower is in the shed now. I run it for five minutes every few weeks to keep the damp off. The light is returning. The sun is strengthening and the grass is growing – imperceptibly, but it's growing. It will soon be time to cut it again. We are going to survive our first winter in Orkney.

CHAPTER FOUR

# The Edge of Darkness

I CAUGHT THE island bug when my parents took me on holiday to Arran in 1959. The existence of worlds across water, smaller, self-contained and different was a revelation to me and has remained a fascination ever since.

The dream of living on an island was never fixed. Sometimes there would be a wee boat for the not too difficult crossing to the shops, a seabird study project and a thesis to write by candle-light of an evening. In more realistic moments, the fantasy was an island with a sizeable population, good ferry service and a Tesco.

Realism has prevailed and we've come to Orkney. Don't let the supermarket fool you, though, this is still island life at its very best. There are over 20,000 people here but everyone is my neighbour. Orkney has an international airport, state-of-the-art schools and a state-of-the-art hospital opened in 2019. There is theatre, cinema, music, sport, shopping, eating out, care for the elderly and support for everyone who needs it.

None of the above is the picture postcard island of the imagination. We don't send cards to friends showing the airport or the hospital building site. They are not what we came for but they are, most definitely, what make it possible and comfortable to live here.

The greeting card views are here though. On some mornings and evenings, the sky blazes gold, red and orange or rages black and grey. The sea froths and foams and shines in a gale or sparkles like glass. There are bird flocks, meadows, lochs and Stone Age treasures that will take your breath away.

The community is very strong. Any excuse is taken to get together for tea, home bakes and a natter. The venues and activities vary but the outcome is always the same. 'Whit like the day?

(How are you today?) is the standard greeting. After a few months here, I was struggling to place all the faces I recognised, who they were and where I knew them from. If I spend a split second too long staring and wondering then the person opposite will nod and smile, probably wondering the same thing.

I drove north until I could drive no further, then took ship and got off when it stopped. I drove to the shore and built a house. At night, I walk Dog down the lane to where the streetlights end – at the edge of darkness. If the night is still and clear I gaze out at lights on Hoy and Flotta, on ships and rocks in the Flow, and wait for Duncansby Head lighthouse to flash, 20 miles away on the Scottish mainland. There is no need to go any further.

CHAPTER FIVE

# Moving Day

'DO YOU WANT today's paper or yesterday's?' enquired the girl behind the counter at the newsagent. 'Because if it's today's you're after you'll have to come back tomorrow.'

Island life is different, I already knew that, but this was just one small further example of it. I left the shop chuckling and pleased at the thought that neither I nor the paper seller really minded the slight inconvenience.

I had wanted the paper so I could read about everything that happened in the world on the day I moved to live in Orkney. It was Thursday 17 August 2017. No matter, tomorrow will be fine, I thought.

The second most commonly asked question of me is, 'What on Earth is behind your fascination with islands?' The first is, 'What is your favourite island?' Impossible. There are so many, they're all different, each with their own character and charms.

Neither question is easy. I grew up by the sea in East Yorkshire and believe the sea to be in my blood – it was certainly in my bed on the stormiest nights, when spray sometimes drifted in through the open window, or bubbled up under the sash. When the tide was far out, we were fascinated and excited, as children, by Stoney Island which appeared briefly. We could walk to it and search for crabs. The WWII Bull Fort, defending the Humber estuary, was a foreboding presence – gloomy, rusting, forbidden but promising adventure if ever we could have landed.

However, I think my analyst, if I had one, would say it was the swimming baths at North Bay, Scarborough that actually burned islands into my psyche one evening in 1959. The pool had islands, you see, and I determined to land on one. I couldn't swim but my rubber ring floated me there and then I dared not slip back into the deep water when it came time to leave. The lifeguard had to be called and I was carried ashore (the water only came up to his waist). Luckily, I haven't needed a lifeguard since that day but, 80 Scottish islands later, the determination to land and the frisson of crossing water has never left me.

Our new house is lovely. Bob Budge did a brilliant job and I should like to record my thanks to him and all his men. He planned ahead at every stage. Stuff needing to come from south often had to be ordered weeks in advance so the project wasn't held up. They called it 'The Critical Path' when I visited the site of the new hospital a few weeks ago. 'We've got the doors and windows home just now,' Bob would say, or 'The bathroom suite is home.' As I write this, the painters are finishing off inside, a few copper pipes need things sticking on the end and Dougie has to sweep up. Grass is sprouting in the garden and I hope the buttercups, clover and orchids have survived the excavations and will return in due course. I am reliably informed that, in the case of the buttercups at least, I need have no worries.

I registered to vote in Scotland. I have my Orkney library card and qualify for islander travel discounts. I have tickets for the lifeboat dinner dance, a phone number beginning 01856, a KW post code, neighbours, big skies and sea all around. Bob even agreed to install a wood-burning stove in the lounge. 'You can have one if you like,' he said, 'but the insulation in that hoose is so good you'll have to sit in your underpants after you light it.'

I think the attraction of a wood-burner is to satisfy the deep-rooted, Neolithic bit of my subconscious that wants to look at a living flame. I want to provide for us by hunter-gathering wood and berries, and storing both against the long winter nights. I ordered a shed. When Dog and I walk on Scapa Beach, we find a nice washed-up fence post to dry and add to the log pile.

I called in to see Mark Rendall at Rendall Furnishings in the town. 'The beds and carpets you ordered are all home just now. We're ready to fit them when the painters finish,' he said. I'm home too – more at home than any time since those days on Stoney Island.

Wood burning stove – Carlin Skerry.

CHAPTER SIX

# Cooling-off Period

THE MODERN WAY allows a cooling-off period when one signs a contract. We've had 28 days in our Orkney house now, the weather has cooled a bit but we're still keen.

We had our first visitors from south, Jane and Howard, so we've been looking at Orkney afresh, through new eyes. We invited Jane months earlier and told her to bring a friend. She had been on the phone to Howard in Barnsley last Thursday, trying to fix a date for coffee, when she said, 'Actually, do you fancy a few days in Orkney?' Jane set off from Sheffield on Sunday night to pick him up and phoned ahead to see if he was ready. 'I've been ready since just after you rang on Thursday,' he replied.

Howard had always wanted to see the Italian Chapel so we drove out on their first morning. Crossing the barrier, he said, 'That looks like a couple of wartime Nissen huts over there.'

'That's the chapel,' I said. 'We're here.'

'Is that the chapel? Am I really seeing the chapel? I can't believe I'm actually seeing the Italian Chapel having heard about it so many times. My mate, Dave, will be green. "Make sure you see the Italian Chapel," he told me.'

'Wow,' Jane said when we pulled up at Brough of Birsay.

The tide was in, the sun was out and shining on the waves rolling across the causeway, which was visible just below the surface of the clear water, snaking out to the island. We drove back to collect Howard from where we had left him, looking for 400-million-year-old fossils at a disused quarry, had a lunch of crab sandwiches and coffee from Palace Stores in Birsay village and went back to see if the causeway was uncovered – it wasn't.

We agreed to leave Brough of Birsay until their next visit.

'Never mind,' said Howard as we turned the car. 'Look, there's an igneous dyke.' He is a geography and geology teacher and had spotted some dark rock streaking across some lighter rock and declared it to be an igneous intrusion. I find geologists are like that generally, always asking one to believe some impossible thing had happened some inconceivably long time ago. I was still recovering from the fossil fish sitting in the cup holder. Howard could not have been happier.

Jane and Howard left Orkney declaring themselves well satisfied with their introduction to Neolithic stone houses, burial chambers, causeways, history, gannets and bar-tailed godwits. Jane said, 'I do understand why you love it and have chosen to live here, although the pampas grass is not a patch on mine.'

I have a few days off now, before Phil and Maggie arrive. It was quite difficult to refocus after the others left so I just did some ironing and dozed in the armchair for a bit. The shed was delivered, in sections, on Friday. Bev can't wait for it to be erected so that all the tools, bikes, storage boxes, mower, cycle carriers and snorkel gear can be cleared out of the end room, allowing the furniture to be set up. Sadly we now have to wait for a dry, calm day, which doesn't look imminent.

I have found myself to be more patient with the weather, however, than when I was only here for a limited time. Saturday was glorious, I had just arrived at Scapa, the tide was way out and I was looking forward to a long walk. A phone call diverted me to an urgent task so I missed the beach. Driving away, I consoled myself with the thought the sand and shells would all be there on every sunny day in the future.

Our house is on the edge of the village, just inside the farthest extent of the streetlights. This may limit our appreciation of the stars a bit and might make viewing the Mirrie Dancers (northern lights) more difficult, but it does mean that darkness dog-walking is less challenging. I can walk down the lane, heading due south towards Scapa Flow. In the daylight, I can see Barrel of Butter, Flotta and Cava but at night I know them only by their lights. As I reach the post signing the end of 30 miles an hour I can look out into darkness. It is like standing on the prow of a ship, butting through the Atlantic waves, at times.

At others, it is truly calm and the moon lights the way across to the other islands.

I've been writing this on Sunday afternoon. The rain has just stopped beating on the glass and the wind has ceased whistling round the eaves. The sky over Hoy has brightened. The sun is coming out. Time to walk the dog before the next lot of weather blows in.

## CHAPTER SEVEN
# The Stress of Moving

THEY SAY THE stress of moving house is on a par with a bereavement or the breakup of a relationship. I'm not sure I would agree, but it can certainly raise the pulse and the blood pressure and deprive one of sleep.

I know exactly to the day, date, hour and minute when the decision to move to Orkney was taken – by my wife, Bev. It had been an almost lifelong hope of mine that I would, one day, live on a Scottish island, but she had taken a lot more convincing. I was resigned to a life south but with long and frequent sojourns north. Then, one day, we were driving past a building site in Orkney.

It was Sunday, the builder was away. The house was almost ready for occupation. I had seen inside a few days earlier and knew the plot next door was for sale too.

'Come and look in this house,' I said, 'No pressure – just out of interest.'

'I can't do that, they'll think I'm trying to steal it,' Bev said.

It being Orkney, the house was unlocked. Expensive builders' power tools were lying around but we had the place to ourselves.

'I'll just look through the door, but I'm not going inside.'

Our voices echoed though the uncarpeted space. There was a smell of sawdust. Light flooded through the south facing windows and the sea glittered beyond. From the porch we could see through the hall – there were no internal doors at that stage – into the kitchen, to what looked like some smart new units. Bev's curiosity got the better of her and she went to have a look. Emboldened, now, she left the kitchen and went along the hall to the lounge, bathroom and bedrooms beyond. Two minutes later, she was back and I will never forget what came next.

'Let's buy it,' she said. 'Not this one but the plot next door. We can have one built while I finish off some work in the south, then move in.'

By teatime on the Monday, we had put in an offer for the land, visited the council planning department and the roads department (to see if access would be a problem), the electricity board (to see where power could be got) and started looking up builders. Bev does not let grass grow once her mind is made up. The landowner was not in a hurry to sell and there was some suspicion that he had earmarked it for a family member. 'I'll be gutted now if we don't get it,' Bev said.

We seemed to be on the tenterhooks for some time. A meeting with the landowner in Kirkwall had to be postponed when the cruise ship I was working on failed to land in bad weather. We eventually met in Edinburgh and he agreed to give our offer 'careful consideration'. Some weeks later (by coincidence on the deck of another cruise ship), the acceptance arrived by email. Under Scottish law, such an undertaking is binding so celebrations were had.

I had been amazed how welcoming, accommodating and unsuspicious the various local officials had been. There had been no making of appointments, presentation of documents or uttering of passwords as I'm sure there would have been in other places. At the electricity board, the receptionist simply shouted across the open plan office to see if anyone could help us. A young man (he seemed to be about 12) with the largest computer screen I had ever seen shouted back that he had a few minutes. It was only when he stood up to shake hands that I could see him over the screen.

'Where is the property?' he asked. He quickly had the village on his screen. I could see the kirk, the school and the footprints of several houses. 'Can you point to your plot?' he said. That done, he zoomed in and I could see the end of the houses next door on each side, a bit of road and a fence line. Home.

The close-up picture showed every underground cable, water pipe, drain, telephone cable and even the remains of a disused well. There may have been a Neolithic settlement below that but I can't swear to it.

'Look, here's a transformer that might do,' he said, warming to the task. He clicked on the transformer and a red line drew itself to the centre of the plot. '200m exactly,' he said. 'It'll cost £7,327–49 to run power from there.' I can't recall whether VAT was extra but it was a very useful guide. 'You may be able to talk to the people on the other side and get a shorter (hence cheaper) supply.'

That seemed very easy and straightforward. Jump on a few months – the plot has been bought, the plans approved, the builder is ready to start and the cable has been laid to the plot. In the end, we did manage to negotiate a shorter route. I phoned a Well Known Electricity Supplier – known as WKES for short. Here is a verbatim transcript of our conversation – honest. Please note: during the conversation one of the customer service agents actually said, 'Certainly, Mr Clubley, that's absolutely no problem at all.'

How to Install an Electricity Meter at Your New House

**Me:** [Dialling WKES on 03450724318]

**Automated Response (AR):** This number has been changed to 03450724319.

**Me:** [Dialling 03450724319)]

**Agent 001:** Hello, WKES, how may I help you today?

**Me:** Hello, I'd like to request the installation of a new meter please.

**Agent 001:** Sorry, you need to contact an electricity supplier.

**Me:** But isn't WKES an electricity supplier?

**Agent 001:** Yes, but there are two separate companies, we are the other part of WKES, sorry. Dial 03450262658.

**Me:** [Dialling 03450262658]

**Agent 002:** Hello, WKES, how may I help you today?

**Me:** I'd like to request the installation of a new meter please.

**Agent 002:** Sorry, you need to dial 03450737721.

**Me:** [Dialling 03450737721]

**Agent 003:** Hello, WKES, how may I help you today?

**Me:** I'd like to request the installation of a new meter please.

**Agent 003:** Certainly, can I take the address? Are there any cats and dogs at the address? Do you want Credit, Quarterly Billing or Pay as you Go?

**Me:** What's the difference between Credit and Quarterly Billing?

**Agent 003:** They're the same thing, sorry, I should have said Credit (aka Quarterly Billing) or Pay as you Go.

**Me:** Credit please.

**Agent 003:** *Certainly Mr Clubley, that's absolutely no problem at all.* Is it commercial or domestic?

**Me:** Domestic.

**Agent 003:** Sorry, this is the wrong department, I'll transfer you.

**Me:** I'd like to request the installation of a new meter please.

**Agent 004:** No problem. We'll do it on 27 February, can someone be at the property? Where is the meter to be sited?

**Me:** On the end of the cable that's already sticking up. We need a Temporary Building Supply Meter.

**Agent 004:** Ah, that's a different procedure, I'll have to send you some forms.

Five days later, the forms arrive…

**The form read:** 'Every question must be answered or there will be a delay.'

**Q1–4 on the form:** What are the VT ratio, MCP, DA and DC required?

**Me:** Hi again, 004. I don't understand question 1–4 on the form.

**Agent 004:** Oh, don't worry about those questions.

**Me:** But it says there'll be a delay if I don't answer them.

**Agent 004:** No there won't. Who will be at the property to let the engineer in?

**Me:** It's just a building plot – there's nothing on it except a cable sticking up and the meter is to go on the end of that cable.

**Agent 004:** But someone has to be there to let the engineer in.

**Me:** But there is no fence or gate… He can just pull off the road and walk to where he sees the cable sticking up.

**Agent 004:** But someone has to…

Two weeks and 600 miles later, I was in Orkney to let the engineer in. I had sold the idea of the trip to Bev as 'ESSENTIAL PROJECT MANAGEMENT, dear, I need to be there.' I could do a bit of birdwatching, walking and generally enjoying our soon-to-be new home. I stayed in the apartment we had rented for just such an eventuality. I know I could have prevailed on someone locally to be there but this was more fun.

It was a wonderful time, learning how to live in Orkney, playing at being a resident even before we were. Bev was never too keen on the apartment. The shower and toilet were private but on a corridor shared with Julie in the apartment opposite.

I watched as the engineer twisted the two ends of cable together and wrapped insulating tape around them (not really).

**Me:** Do I need to be here?

**Engineer:** No

**Me:** Did I ever need to be here?

**Engineer:** No

For WKES, however, read any utility company. The Well Known Phone Company (WKPC) made and cancelled four separate appointments to come and twist their bits of wire to ours. Eventually I discovered one of their senior staff in the area was a neighbour so I asked him to intervene. Next day I looked out to see a WKPC van outside, then another. I pulled on my clothes and went outside, by which time there were three WKPC vans – parked next door.

'Hooray,' I said. 'Have you come to install my phone?'

'No mate,' one of them said in a north of England accent. 'Next door.'

'But next door already have a phone,' I explained.

'Hang on a minute – stop diggin' that trench Dave – we're at the wrong house, it's this bloke 'ere we want.'

'Where have you come from?'

'Blackpool. We're here for four days, plus the two days travelling at either end. We've no idea where we are with these country addresses. That's why we got the wrong house. What made you choose to live in Orkney anyway?'

'I had the choice of here or Blackpool.'

He seemed to enjoy the joke. They were great lads. I was so pleased to see them I drove into Kirkwall and got them fish and chips.

In conversations with WKES, WKPC and the others I repeatedly asked why, since they spent their days and weeks installing meters and phones etc, they hadn't bothered to sit down and work out quick, efficient ways of doing it, so they could have longer tea breaks. You may have noticed all customer service operatives have been taught to deflect criticism by agreeing with everything the complainant says, so they all agreed with me.

In fact, there was only one really big stress involved in the move. It was the one where we almost ran out of money to pay the builder because we didn't sell the old house and move into rented before starting the building as we should have done.

I kept telling the people at WKES and WKPC that I was retired, this was the only house I was ever going to build so I was quite cool about the endless delays. I just felt sorry for them, going through it with every customer, as they surely must – being in want of a good system, as they clearly were. However, if I did ever do it all again, I would sell first, get the money in the bank and then let the diggers roll in – even if I had to sleep in a tent.

There were lots of little stresses though. They seem like nothing now but, day after day, they lead to slight fraying of the nerves and testing of relationships. Here are just a few:

Supermarkets don't save cardboard boxes anymore. They crush and pack them straight away as they are a fire hazard, so we had nothing to pack our stuff in. At one Well Known Super Store (WKSS), however, they are not a fire hazard – perfectly safe in fact – and can be stacked under the display counter for customers to use. I started collecting banana boxes but made the mistake of sharing the tip with a pal, who was also moving. Soon there were few boxes to be had and this was a source of stress. We did, eventually, get enough – about 200 I think – and they were brilliant for the job. Months later as we unpacked, we had 200 banana boxes to collapse and take to the recycling centre – a daily chore.

I had thought it would be nice to truly recycle them so I made some labels that read: 'This box has carried bananas from the Caribbean to Sheffield and then personal possessions from Sheffield to Orkney, please record below what you use it for then pass it on.'

My plan was to save them all up and advertise them, free, on the Orkney buy and sell website. Sadly, giving over an entire room in the new house to hoard boxes was too stressful so they went to the skip – labels and all.

Four weeks before we moved in, I injured my foot walking into a pub (I know – *into* the pub). I misjudged the step, put all my weight down on a half-supported foot and did my Achilles tendon. When I had subsequently lived in Orkney for six months, someone asked me how it was going. 'Every step I have taken in Orkney has been painful,' I said.

The ground round the house was building site mud. There was no fence around it, so Dog couldn't be let loose on it for fear she would run away. On the lead was fine – apart from the mud brought into the house on her paws. The grass grew quite quickly in the end and the fence man soon had the job done. Two more stresses eased.

In the days and weeks following the move, the house was transformed into a home. Each night we could sit down in more comfort and with more things organised than the night before. I spent the first few days fixing pictures, mirrors, curtains, cabinets, shelves, vacuum cleaners, coat pegs, toilet roll holders and televisions to the wall.

We accelerated the clearing of space by selling stuff – rocking chair, lawn mower, microwave oven, washing machine and tumble dryer – on the local website. Then we found we still needed the lawn mower to reach the corners the big, new one couldn't, so I had to buy another.

I guess you must be getting a bit bored with my little stresses by now. You must be thinking I'm making mountains out of mole-hills. Maybe I am, but the point I would make is that this is all with hindsight. I can assure you that it was only a few weeks of not knowing the grass would get cut, the shed would get erected and dry out inside, the mould that had appeared inside would not cause it to fall down. I bought a dehumidifier, a humidity meter and some fungicide but, come the spring, the shed dried out. It's like an oven now when the sun is on it – we dry towels in there. I have a dehumidifier, humidity meter and fungicide I don't need. The guest room would be cleared, the leak in the gutter would be fixed, the plumber would come and finish the stove flue.

We snapped and snarled at each other through the early days until one day we sat down and said, 'Enough.' We drew deep breaths and pledged to be kinder. We were and soon the stresses began to take on the right proportions and fade.

In 2018, we celebrated one year in the house. I cannot recall a year passing so quickly. All the challenges of the previous 365 days were met and solved or survived. Things started to come round again: choir practice began for another autumn; the surgery got the flu vaccine again; nights drew in and early evening sun fell on our back step again – just as it had on our first night. We already knew where to put the Christmas tree when the time came.

Dustbins, Carlin Skerry – illegally secured against the wind.

CHAPTER EIGHT

# Like Sleeping Whales

'CAN YOU SEE trees from your new house in Orkney?' a friend, Iain, asked the other day.

I thought for a moment, picturing the low, rolling hills to the north and the green, sheep-flecked fields sloping down to the sea in the south.

'Yes, there are a few, planted for shelter round a biggish house by the shore.' I was relieved to have remembered a few but I suspected not enough to deflect the reservation I knew was coming. I was right.

'You see, I wouldn't like that, I like trees around me,' Iain said.

I went away and pondered this. It's true, of course: Orkney doesn't have many trees. I love trees but I have never missed them in Orkney. The islands have been described as 'sleeping whales', low, smooth hills lying at rest in the water. This has been seen as an attractive thing, a mark of beauty. Sleeping whales are not bristly, so trees would spoil this particular picture. Actually, on a visit south after we'd been here a few months, I found myself driving along between hedgerows feeling frustrated at not being able to see around.

Then I got to thinking about why there are so few trees. The answer is not a simple one. After the last ice age, 11,000 years ago, the land was colonised by plants which, eventually, led to a climax vegetation of woodland. They were not towering oaks or pines. More likely a covering of scrubby alder, hazel, birch, rowan, ash and others.

The location of the islands, exposed to Atlantic gales, probably limited further succession but Orkney had its woods. It still has a few. Berriedale Wood in north Hoy is officially Britain's most northerly natural woodland. A few of the aforementioned species huddle in a gully between Orkney's only mountains. Berriedale has been there for centuries but does not appear to be expanding out of the gully. The reasons for the decline of Orkney's trees are complicated. Experts talk of paludification (look it up) and other technical things, but wind and humans with stone axes get the most column inches.

The New Stone Age, or Neolithic, is celebrated in Orkney like nowhere else in Britain. When the first farmers came here, around 5,000 years ago, they built the most wonderful houses, villages, burial chambers and mysterious stone circles. A modern visitor can, in a comfortable day, see the houses at Skara Brae, the burial mound at Maeshowe and the Ring of Brodgar, and still have time for tea in Kirkwall, a look round the cathedral and a bit of souvenir shopping.

The men with axes lived at Skara Brae and similar villages. We know this for certain because we have found some of the axes that chopped down Orkney's trees. They are treasures now, with many in the museums. People come from all over the world to marvel at them.

It may be that the trees were in decline before the Neolithic. It could be that the intensive use of stone (rather than wood) for building during Orkney's Stone Age was precisely *because* of the timber shortage. That the fabulous structures have survived may be down to the relative lack of disturbance and intensive agriculture found elsewhere in Britain. Whatever, we have super stone structures, but not so many trees. Orkney is wonderful, but not like the mythical Sherwood.

One of the things I love about the UK is we have Orkney *and* woods. That said, there is nothing to stop us planting a few trees now. Some people are experimenting with coppiced willow crops as a renewable fuel. Perhaps not everyone's idea of a woodland glade but better than nothing surely. I think what few woodlands there are in Orkney are being better cared for and people think a lot more about the opportunities for planting.

I was once birdwatching on Fair Isle when someone said, 'There's a scarlet rosefinch resting in the bushes outside the shop. Give the bushes a shake and it might show itself.'

That was 20 years ago and I have always remembered it as a most unsympathetic thing to do. That tired and hungry bird had found a landfall and shelter after who knows how many hundreds of miles of open sea and someone was happy to disturb it for another tick in his book. But I also remember how tiny the clump of mini-trees was, yet still useful to the bird. It was actually in a planticrub. When I get to planning our Orkney garden next year, there will be as many shrubs and bushes as we can manage, commensurate with retaining a view of the sea, plus thistles and all manner of seedy bird food plants. I'm hoping a scarlet rosefinch will come and stay a few days.

*Primula scotica* – the Scottish primrose, a rare Orkney gem.

CHAPTER NINE

# Walking the Dog

WE'VE ARRIVED – Martin, the local vicar, has written our names in his book.

'I meet so many people,' he told me, 'I have to keep a note of who they are in this little book.'

'That book's replaced his brain,' said his lady, 'he'd be lost without it.'

We have bought land and built a house. We are to invest in Orkney and she will invest in us. Our first instalment was an entry in the vicar's book. I was sitting with the minister, and others, in the weekly community coffee morning where, for just £1, one can enjoy coffee, a home bake and a good blether. The kirk is five minutes from home and, as a lover of cakes (but probably beyond redemption), I'm sure I'll be back most Thursdays.

'We're Presbyterian here,' he said.

'Well, I must confess to being lapsed Methodist,' I told him.

'Oh, don't worry, there's plenty of time.'

Down the side of the kirk, the quiet lane leads to the shore, and this has become a regular dog walk. There's almost no traffic and the cliff top is soon reached. I can make a circular walk back to the house by turning left or right onto the cliff path but left is favourite, as it involves less road walking.

In the summer, the narrow strip of maritime heath, squeezed in between the cliff top and the fields, is a joy. There are ling and bell heathers, tormentil, eyebright, thrift, clover, buttercup, hogweed, thistles, lady's finger and others beyond my ken. Fulmars patrol at eye-level and a bonxie (great skua) keeps an eye on them, like a security supervisor at a football match. The narrow path is insufficiently trodden to be much more than a sheep track. In wet weather, ankles are soon soaked from swishing against the heathers.

The walk drops down to sea level. This is a little-visited part of Orkney and odd bits of nylon rope have washed ashore, lost overboard from boats or fish farms (my walk is not included in the annual, community efforts that maintain cleanliness on more popular beaches). In two or three passages, however, I collected everything that was there, carried or dragged it to the road for collection later and transfer to the 'Pick Up Three' collection bin sponsored by local school children.

I have appointed myself Guardian of the Path. I reckon I'll be able to keep it more or less clean with a few regular walks. Who knows? I might even find a barrel of brandy, lump of ambergris, message in a bottle or see a killer whale. Even without the rare sightings, the walk and the conservation work are deeply satisfying and I look forward to more of them.

The path soon reaches an old pier, with a super beach just beyond. Sandy beaches are often thought of as August places but when there's an R in the month this is a great spot for flocks of golden plover, redshank, long-tailed duck, curlew and a supporting cast of ringed plover, shag, cormorant, eider ducks, common and grey seals. There's a seat on the pier, sheltered from the wind, and a good place from which to watch. Sitting here for half an hour is as good as an NHS prescription for a course of mindfulness, I reckon. I would ask for my half hour on the NHS but, like all of life's best, it's already free at the point of use.

The farm track carries me back up to my starting height and views over Scapa Flow that take in almost everything, from Hoxa Head and the main entrance to the Flow, Flotta and the Oil Terminal and round to Hoy. Stromness can't be seen but I *can* see the headland behind which the little town is hiding.

Beuy, what a place. Orkney really is somewhere special – wildflowers, birds, sea – and landscapes. There's so much history out in the Flow. There's archaeology almost back to the ice age and telemetry on hill tops listening to satellites. They're harnessing the waves and tides is driving progress. Life on the edge is exciting.

The track gives onto the road again for a five-minute walk home with Dog on the lead. The village is fairly new, with infill building making a neat little community. The attractions of Orkney include wide open spaces, big skies, peace and quiet but, after all that, it's nice to have streetlights all the way home as the light fades.

Northern marsh orchid that appeared in our lawn at Carlin Skerry.

CHAPTER TEN

# A Working Landscape

AN ORKNEY FRIEND has just had built a wonderful sun room extension to her house, overlooking the harbour from high on the hillside. I had been waiting, patiently, for several weeks, for a slot to open for lunch so I could help her admire the view from the cushioned window seat. Chilled drinks (with ice cubes) came from the new American fridge; gentle background music drifted down from the built-in speakers (it is a smart room) and draughts were efficiently excluded by the triple-glazed Norwegian windows.

It's at times like this that one studies the landscape anew. Things that had become familiar and largely unseen get re-examined as one experiments with the luxury of the expanded view.

'It is a working landscape,' Caroline said as she pointed out the drained reservoir-turned-builders yard, the work boat placing markers for a new fish farm, the ferries coming and going on the daily shuttle between Kirkwall and the other islands and the inevitable wind turbines.

The previous night I had been standing outside. It was close to midnight, the sky was clear and the air unusually still. After a few minutes of eye adjustment, it became apparent there are far more stars in the heavens than I had previously thought when living south, in the big city. Layer upon layer of ever fainter and ever more distant objects came into focus. I could hear the curlews calling, and the odd oystercatcher protesting as it flew over (oystercatchers are always complaining about something or other).

What little light pollution there is outside the house comes from the oil terminal, six miles away, across Scapa Flow. When the breeze blew towards me, I could just hear the generator hum of a tanker waiting in the Flow to transfer its cargo at the terminal. Would I prefer the terminal and the tanker were not here? I thought. Yes, came my reply, but if they were not here, and if

the turbines, fish farms, builders yards, ferries, radio masts, tar-
mac roads (and road works), dustbin lorries, traffic wardens and
tractors were not here either, then neither would I.

As my friend said, Orkney is a working landscape. (Orkney has
always been a working landscape. The Neolithic folk who built
Skara Brae and Ness of Brodgar left a bit of decoration behind
but, mostly, they left tools.) There are still plenty of square miles
in which to get lost here on high days and holidays – or every day
if one is lucky enough to be retired. There are deserted beaches,
empty moorlands and soaring cliff-top walks but, in between
these fabulous places, there is what we have come to call industry
and infrastructure.

In Orkney, you can do just about anything you might fancy: go
to a concert, the cinema, theatre, play squash, golf, eat out, sail,
dive, knit, blether or just sit quietly in the award-winning library
and read free magazines. You can buy pretty much anything too.
Recently I purchased a pair of boots, some organic muesli, a
wood-burning stove, a 50m builder's tape (from a choice of four)
and a kitchen tap that delivers water at 100°C, thus doing away
with the need for a kettle.

This all adds up to saying Orkney is a comfortable place to
live. Some Scottish islands are picture postcard places and nothing
more. There are beautiful islands home only to millions of seabirds, but I couldn't live there. People have chosen the hermit life
in days past – monks lived in bee-hive cells while shepherds and
their families dwelt on isolated, rocky outcrops. Ronald Lockley,
Frank Fraser Darling, Robert Atkinson and Bryan Nelson have
all, famously, stayed more or less alone on otherwise uninhabited
islands and written about their experiences. Even today, there are
hardy souls living on Auskerry (2) and Vaila in Shetland (2) but
they are a rare and possibly endangered breed.

Within living memory, there are islands in Orkney – Swona, Cava,
Faray, Fara – that have been lived on, but no more. People loved the
way of life but the most common reason for abandonment was that
life was easier on the bigger island.

'I would go back tomorrow if I could take my washing machine,' said one lady, shortly after leaving Stroma for life on the Caithness mainland.

In the end, the working landscape is a safe and comfortable place to live. I will continue to seek out empty beaches, cliff tops and moors. I will take deep breaths of fresh sea air. I will collect shells, watch birds and enjoy flowers. There are places in Orkney I can walk all day and not meet another soul but, when I need a new tap washer, internet connection or a takeaway curry – well, I can have them too.

Peeping through the window of a deserted house.

## CHAPTER ELEVEN

# Home Bakes

A FEW YEARS ago, I was wandering on Stromness pier one Sunday afternoon when I met a group of young lads doing the same. We passed the time of day for a while and they told me they liked living in Orkney 'because [they] are free'. They were too young to have arrived at that idea themselves, I thought. They surely hadn't experienced the other side of life enough to have made the conclusion on their own. It is an idea handed down by older generations in islands but no less valid for that.

I was writing a piece about the Stromnessian author George Mackay Brown at the time so I asked the boys what they knew of him. 'He wrote poems,' said one. 'He had blue eyes,' said another. 'There's a painting of him hanging in our school.'

I asked if they still fished for sillocks from the pier, as George had done in his youth. 'Oh, yes, we give them to people for their cats,' they replied. They were shocked to learn that GMB and friends had sold them 'to wives with cats, four for a penny'. Orkney youngsters must be a lot better off these days as the thought had not occurred to them.

The spirit of young enterprise is, however, alive and well at Craigiefield Park, Kirkwall, where Allisia Burton runs The Peedie Bun Box. 'I love baking,' Allisia told me. 'My dad teased me about it and suggested I open my own business – so I did. I designed the Bun Box and Dad [Albert] made it in his shed.' The Peedie Bun Box, gaily painted blue and white to resemble a beach hut, operates an honesty system outside the Burtons' home. Whenever Allisia gets a break, she fills it with home bakes and gives a shout out to her regular customers on Facebook. She also does special charity bakes for MacMillan Cancer Support and Maggie's Family Cancer Support in Aberdeen. Allisia is determined to own and operate her own bakery one day. I wouldn't bet against her.

The honesty box is a feature of island life I have long admired. Stories are legion, like the Shetland bus shelter with all mod-cons and the Kerrera phone box, at the pier, where shopping is left for folk to collect.[1] Honesty has to be taught, of course. Respect for others and for property doesn't just happen; it is learned at a young age.

Nowhere have I seen a better example of such a lesson than at the Höfn youth club in Westray. Höfn is an Old Norse word meaning 'harbour' or 'place of safety', an excellent name, I thought, for an Orkney youth club. The building was provided by Westray Development Trust funding at the time of the millennium and has been in good use ever since. The unique feature of the Höfn, as a youth club, is that there is no adult supervision. Every eligible youngster on Westray (aged 12–17) has a swipe card for the door and they can come and go freely. 'It's open 24/7,' one of the girls told me. 'You could sleep there if you wanted to – but I don't think anyone has yet. We have games consoles and stuff. No one would steal them. What would be the point? Everyone would know who'd done it.' I went to have a look at the Höfn. It was clean, tidy and orderly. I left wondering why the same principles of trust can't transfer to our big cities.

---

[1] Someone once ordered a bottle of whisky. It was still there, in the phone box, three days later when he collected it.

CHAPTER TWELVE

# A House by Any One of Several Names

WE HAD TO choose a name for our new house. In January 2017, we turned over the first sod on the plot in Orphir and the next task was to dig a trench to bring in the electricity supply. A temporary meter had been installed so Bob, the builder, could use his power tools on site. No such luxury was afforded the builders of Skara Brae or Ness of Brodgar but then they probably didn't have impatient customers like me saying 'When can we move in Bob?' Then again, perhaps they did. Archaeologists seem to agree, however, that for Neolithic monument builders, the *process* was the main thing – they just built without any clear idea of what the finished thing would look like, or even when it *was* finished. I reminded Bob to stick to the plan, we're not quite ready for a chambered tomb yet. A hot-stone sauna might have been quite nice though.

From the plot I can look out over Scapa Flow and the curiously named Barrel of Butter, just off shore. Barrel of Butter is a low, wave-washed islet, a major hazard to shipping were it not for its light tower. From a distance it looks not unlike a surfaced submarine and was indeed mistaken for one, and shelled, during WWI.

The name Barrel of Butter comes from the practice in olden times of locals paying one barrel of butter per annum to the landowner in return for the right to hunt seals there. The rent had originally been a barrel of seal oil but, as seals became scarcer, it was reduced to butter.

Barrel of Butter appears as the name of the rock on maps and charts at least as far back as 1761 but it was originally known as Carlin Skerry, a name which also appears alongside Barrel of

Butter on Admiralty charts as recently as 1920 and 1944. Carlin is defined as an old woman, hag or witch in a variety of sources. There are several references to it in the literature, not least in Burns' *Tam O' Shanter:*

> They reel'd, they set, they crossed, they cleekit
> Till ilka carlin swat and reekit

(They danced till all the women sweated and smelled, basically.)

Jaqueline Riding, in her excellent 2016 book, *Jacobites*, describes an encounter between Charles Edward Stuart, disguised as a maid and a member of Flora Macdonald's family. She did not recognise the prince and cried out:

> such a muckle Trollop of a Carling make sick lang Strides
> through the Hall.

Old Norse has the word *kerling* which I checked with Dr Ragnhild Ljosland at Kirkwall's Centre for Nordic Studies. *Kerling* means, similarly, old woman, ogress or witch. The derivation of the word, however, is the masculine *karl* meaning a free man.

On a much gentler note, the word *carlin* also denoted the last sheaf cut at harvest, or the corn dolly made from it. Carlin heather is bell heather and gorse is also carlin spurs. Bell heather grows in profusion around Orkney and there's a nice showing on the Orphir cliff top overlooking Carlin Skerry.

So, after much deliberation, we decided to call the house Carlin Skerry. We very much wanted it to have an authentic, local name (Cava, Barrel of Butter, Kirk Field and Skiran were all considered, plus an assortment of bird and flower names). With Carlin Skerry, we can think of ourselves as Witch House, Heather House, Gorse House, Sheaf House, Corn Dolly House or Freedom House, depending on mood. We will be preserving an old word by using it and it will make a good talking point for visitors.

Carlin Skerry and foreground poppies.

## CHAPTER THIRTEEN

# Every Day I Pinch Myself

IN MY FORMER life in the south, I had a dream chest. This chest was a set of wide, shallow, oak drawers, like the ones navigators and surveyors use to keep their charts flat. In each drawer was a plan. Every night, after getting into bed I would select a dream, pull it out and examine it for the umpteenth time.

The top drawer held plans to have a bothy by the sea in Orkney, with thick, silent walls, a wood burning stove, original art on the wall and a few other of modern life's accoutrements. Further down was a scheme to have a peedie boat and explore the islands of Scapa Flow. I planned to land on Cava, clean the beach of marine litter, have a campfire and a barbeque.

Opening another drawer revealed ambitions for a best-seller about a man who went to live on an island to be at peace and one with nature.

After that the charts got a bit fanciful – be a lifeboat crew member or win a top prize for travel literature. The chest was not beside the bed, as you might imagine, but in my head.

Now here I am. Bev and I live in Orphir Village. The only downside of moving to Orkney is that the dream chest is looking decidedly empty. It's getting difficult to fantasise because I'm actually here living it. Apart from the lifeboat shouts, for which I'm too old and stiff, I'm doing a lot of what I dreamed of. Now, as I turn out the light, I can say to Bev:

'That was great today, helping Scottish Natural Heritage count terns on Holm of Houton. It was lovely to be exploring an uninhabited island again.'

'Dog and I had a great time on Scapa Beach this morning. The tide was just right for her to walk out into deep water on the outflow pipe and then swim back.'

'The flowers on the clifftop are fabulous just now. I can't keep up with identifying them all, there's a new one in bloom every day.'

'Wasn't the Folk Festival brilliant? Three concerts in four nights – I'm exhausted.'

'Who were your favourites?' she might reply.

'Now you're asking. I couldn't pick one. Gnoss, Fara, String Sisters – they were all great.'

'Yes, they were. Good night, dear.'

The second drawer down – remember, the one with the hope of having a peedie boat – was emptied recently when I travelled up to Shetland and bought one from a man in Whalsay.

I sailed up on MV *Hrossey* from Kirkwall at midnight and arrived in Lerwick, just as I was finishing breakfast in the Feast Restaurant at 7.30 the next morning. I slept on a reclining chair in the cinema (one is allowed to do this after the last film show has finished). There were 20 or more of us in there but everyone was very quiet.

The man picked me up from the pier and after coffee in Lerwick we made the half-hour drive to Laxa for the short crossing to Whalsay. The sea outside the harbour was calm for my test run in the boat. There were puffins on the water, quite close, the first I had seen of the season. With the purchase agreed, I spoke to a van driver in the ferry queue and cadged a lift back to Lerwick. Sleeping on floors, breakfast on boats, hitch-hiking – the day reminded me of all the days I have spent exploring Scotland's islands. It was perfect.

*Hrossey* had kindly waited all day for me to conclude business and she was full for the return run to Kirkwall at teatime and then south to Aberdeen. There was a constant queue for dinner and at the bar. Every available square inch of floor space was occupied by the Shetland Junior Inter County sports teams. Blue track suit tops declaring allegiance to Shetland Hockey, Shetland Athletics and Shetland Swim Team were everywhere. The atmosphere was brilliant (if noisy). The youngsters were excited to be travelling to Orkney for the weekend to do battle in the most keenly fought of annual encounters.

*Hrossey* reached the pier at Kirkwall, early, at around 10.15pm. The June night sky was red and reflected in the water. Gaggles of athletes stood around on the top deck, oblivious to the cold air in which they had been raised. I was taking the last boat home. No one ever arrived home in more glorious surroundings.

CHAPTER FOURTEEN

# A New Way of Walking

I DROVE NORTH on the first day of spring. I've tried various ways of reaching Orkney from my old home in Derbyshire. There's the drive to Aberdeen and ferry (a long day and arrival past bedtime); flying (can't take the dog or crates of tranclements[1]); drive to Caithness and ferry (one very long day or two short ones).

I don't care how I get here. To reach the most sublime places on Earth you have to make an effort. Time is not such a pressure these days so I opt for the two-day drive. Dog and I have our traditional comfort breaks at Scotch Corner, the Cedar Café, then Perth A9 Travelodge (they have a dog-friendly Vintage Inn next door and the whole experience makes a pleasant break).

The second day brings breakfast at the Newtonmore Grill where I once sat outside in glorious sun and a temperature of −4°C, surrounded by snow-covered mountains. Dog likes Golspie Beach and there's a nice sun trap at Golspie Inn.

And, of course, we're in the Highlands now. This trip is not to be rushed in any season. The autumn colours and snowy hills are my favourites. Roads are quieter then too. The causeways at Cromarty Firth and Dornoch Firth are definite waypoints. We are in such open country now that these bridges have cut many miles off the journey. They wouldn't look out of place in Alaska.

No matter how well the driving goes, I am still exhausted on boarding MV *Hamnavoe* in Scrabster for the crossing to Stromness. The freshly cooked fish, chips and peas, with a mug of tea, restores energy. The pager I am given as I order (to tell me when it's ready) would wake the dead, which is just as well as I regularly nod off with the early motion of the boat.

---

1 Tranclements means bits and pieces, treasures, ornaments etc. Thanks to Pauline Welsh for this word.

On previous trips, before we lived in Orkney, I have checked the progress of the daffodils to see whether I could expect flowers before I left. Early in 2017, it looked promising but I'm not so anxious. I live in Orkney so, from now, I'll catch the daffs no matter how late or early. We may even have some of our own. I won't miss the Ba'[2] either or the Folk Festival or St Magnus Festival or flowers in the cathedral or the northern lights or the big tides or the whales...

Orkney is unique. So many of our dormitory towns and high streets in the south are clones. Not Orkney. In Orkney, we will live cheek by jowl with nature, with the weather, with our food production and our energy supply. We know our neighbours, are on first name terms with our shopkeeper and the men who built our house.

Already I am starting to think and feel differently though. Having finished writing *Orkney – A Special Place* (Luath Press, 2014), I was doing some work for someone else. My time is not entirely my own anymore and I find myself driving from A to C and passing B without looking. Hang on a minute, B is world famous and I passed it without thinking. I've never done that before. I begin to worry I will cease to notice the treasures that have, thus far, drawn me back to Orkney again and again.

I don't think so. How can one fail to see the ever-changing sky, the morphing sea? The sound and feel of the wind as it practises its scales across the lumb demand attention. We have come to live in a farming community where the calendar is marked by the comings and goings in the fields. The soil warms and dries and the grass runs through 50 shades of green in a season. Fifty shades a day more like, as the sun brightens or the clouds darken the land.

---

2 The Ba' is street ball game played in Kirkwall on Christmas Day and New Year's Day. Two teams – the Uppies and the Doonies – contest to get a ball to a goal. The Doonies' goal is the harbour basin while the Uppies aim for a wall at the other end of town. Teams can be any size. There are no rules but it is expected that 'fair play' will be observed.

It feels as though we live under a Perspex dome in the city. We still get weather in town, of course, but it is muted and diluted. We are cossetted, blindfolded and sheltered from most of it. Most of the wildlife is something we drive out to the countryside to see, along with the sheep and cows. Here the dome is removed, the air is raw. It is whatever blows in from the sea – the icy cold, the stinging sleet or the burning sun and gentle breeze. Nothing is filtered through dust or slowed by tower blocks. We are like travellers to Mars who have stepped out of the pod to walk on the surface.

Buzz Aldrin said he was too busy on the surface of the moon to gaze around. 'We had practised so much on Earth it all looked familiar anyway,' he said. I intend to look around in Orkney.

## CHAPTER FIFTEEN

# Progress and a Changing View

I RENTED A studio apartment just outside Kirkwall for the dura-
tion of the house build. It was brilliant. It meant I could come to
Orkney as required, without notice, to consult the builder. It was a
lounge/kitchen/diner on the first floor above a garage (quiet) plus
a small bedroom and bathroom along the (shared) landing. There
was frosted glass in the door to the landing and in Julie's door
opposite, so I learned to check if her light was on in the middle
of the night before dashing to the loo in a state unbecoming of a
serious author. I never got caught.

The apartment was unfurnished so I just moved in with my
camping gear for the summer. The bedroom was dark and gloomy
so I put the airbed in the lounge and used the bedroom as a store.
I could bring a van load of stuff from Derbyshire and store it
against the big move. We could also order stuff and have it delivered there in advance. By the day of the move, the bedroom/store
was filled from wall to wall and floor to ceiling. The bathroom
was full of plants and Julie kindly kept them watered during my
absences. The view was over Scapa Beach and already Orkney
was feeling like home.

Bob erected a tea hut for his men to shelter and take their
breaks. He spread out some pallets around the door so they didn't
churn up the mud as they went in and out. His first task on site
had been to lay a substantial hard-core area so vehicles did not do
any churning either. 'Much better to do that first,' he said, 'so we
are not battling the mud as we work.' The ground was not dry.
Nowhere in Orkney was very dry that year but our plot seemed
to be particularly damp. Nevertheless, Bob kept things very tidy,
organised and un-boggy. Two years earlier, the ground was so

wet in Orkney that cattle could not be turned out until July. That was an exception so we were hoping for a drier summer and for building to be completed in comfort.

I organised a fence. The rule in Orkney seems to be that my obligation is to fence things out if I want to, rather than fence things in. Presumably, if I had no objection to my neighbours' sheep and cattle wandering in to eat the dahlias, I wouldn't need a fence. I needed to make the garden safe for Dog anyway. *Rosa rugosa* (rugged rose or Japanese rose) seems to be hardy, an Orkney favourite as a hedging plant, and a few folk promised me as many cuttings as I need. I erected a wire stock fence and then planted stuff in front to make it look better. Rosa, willow and fuchsia should be good. Any other suggestions gratefully received.

Whilst still living in the wooded south, as the trees burst into leaf, I looked at them afresh and wondered how much I'll miss them. A lot of my southern friends have said this would be a problem for them but I think I'll be okay. It'll be nice to visit and have a foliage fix from time to time though. The drive through the Highlands in autumn is as good as that through New England in the fall I reckon, so I'll certainly be planning an October visit to family by road most years. One can't have everything anyway. My favourite view in Orkney is that over Orphir from the top of the road leaving Kirkwall – Scapa Flow and Hobbister moor on the left, Hoy hills in the far distance in front and Kirbister Loch appearing on the right. The sky is never the same twice in this panorama and trees wouldn't improve it one bit. I shall enjoy both at different times.

One shouldn't imagine Orkney to be totally treeless any way. A stand of native Orkney tress huddles in the bottom of a deep cleft between the hills on the way over to Rackwick, from the pier at Moaness. Orkney's native trees are listed as downy birch, hazel, rowan, aspen, willows, roses, honeysuckle and juniper, all having been around since the end of the last ice age around 10,000 years ago. Not mighty oaks but lovely plants for all that, so I need to lower my eyes a bit and see the beauty nearer the ground. I wonder how many of those species I will be able to establish in my hedge.

The problem might be the exposed nature of the site, overlooking Scapa Flow.

While I wait for my forest to mature, I can walk in Binscarth Wood, just outside Finstown, and listen to the songbirds in the spring. There are snowdrops and bluebells too and lots of other things in their season. There's Olav's Wood in South Ronaldsay, created by Helen and Stephen Manson with Olav Dennison back in the 1970s. Olav's is four and a half acres and open for the public to enjoy. It began when Helen asked Olav to help and he started bringing assorted saplings back from trips south. 'These were often self-seeders,' said Olav. 'I was doing people a favour by clearing them out of ditches and the like.'

Orkney's wildlife is fragile. It needs protecting, like wildlife everywhere. I watched a TV series about the Galapagos Islands recently and even that jewel in the world's wild crown is under threat. It will be difficult for me to help Galapagos directly but I'll do whatever I can for Orkney – our own, fabulous archipelago.

## CHAPTER SIXTEEN

# Far North Isn't Far If You Live Here

IT ISN'T FAR to the shops. I popped into the opticians to order some specs the other day and then went along to the surgery for my flu jab. Bev turns out for her morning jog and it's the same distance as a three-mile run at our old home south. She goes to her violin lesson and is back in little more than an hour. Monday's choir practice is a pleasant evening out. There is no sense of being 'remote' or 'a long way from civilisation' or 'at the back of beyond'. We are certainly north of Watford but not out on a limb. It is true, when one contemplates a journey away to visit family and friends, there are cost, time and logistical implications but we live here now. This is the centre of our world and everything is at hand.

I did an evening class: 'Orkney and the Picts' led by Dr Oisín Plumb, lecturer at the Centre for Nordic Studies at the University of Highlands and Islands. How great does that sound? I would have signed up for such a course no matter where I was living but in Orkney, when Oisín talks about Broch of Gurness, it's just up the road and I can go and see it. There are Pictish artefacts in the Orkney Museum too.

The course was actually held in a classroom at Kirkwall Grammar School on Thursday evenings. I loved walking in from the car park. There were always people arriving for other activities, mums and dads collecting or delivering for football training or judo. The all-weather pitch was floodlit and buzzing, and the buzzword is 'community'.

I like to spend an hour, on most days, having coffee or lunch somewhere. I had my favourite spots in the south and have already settled on a few in Orkney. Fare is excellent at Judith Glue's, just across from St Magnus Cathedral. At Judith's, I can sit and look at all the puffin mugs, local foods and knitwear for sale. For a contrast, I go to The Old Library and might hear a rock band tuning up in a venue as modern as any in Edinburgh or London. In Stromness, I frequent Julia's and watch the ferry come and go. Music, memorabilia, modernity or marine scene – what more choice could I wish for with my cappuccino?

We went to the craft fair at Deerness one Sunday afternoon. The Orkney staples of raffle, home bakes and bottomless tea pots were in evidence. Even though a good 15 miles from Orphir, I saw three people I recognised. The trick is to place *where* I knew them from (it was the furniture shop in Kirkwall, the Orphir Community Café and a friend of a friend).

It occurred to me, eating my bacon roll in Deerness and looking round at the folk, I was in the *same* community as the one much closer to home in Orphir. I probably recognised fewer people in Deerness, but they were all still part of the Orkney community. There is an Orcadian way of doing things, of greeting and treating people with a smile and a comment on the weather – 'It's no too bonny oot,' (the weather is poor today). The same was true in Yorkshire and Derbyshire, of course, but I am witnessing it afresh here, with different words and sounds and they are part of what makes them all beautiful places.

## CHAPTER SEVENTEEN

# Stone Ship on Waves of Song

Choir and orchestra, St Magnus Cathedral.

JOCELYN RENDALL likened Orkney's churches to stone ships.[1] I couldn't help thinking of this, sitting in St Magnus Cathedral on the first Sunday in December, listening to the Winter Choir and Orkney Camerata performing works by Vivaldi and Britten. The cathedral is like a stone ship – massive, solid, dependable. If I turn it upside down in my head the roof becomes the keel and the nave the hold – maybe a bit like The Ark. It has carried the souls of a millennium, safely, across the sea of troubles.

---

1 *Steering the Stone Ships: A Story of Orkney Kirks and People*, Jocelyn Rendall (2009)

Over the heads of the violins and cellos were the soprano and alto ladies, gorgeous in their black dresses and red buttonholes. Above them the white-shirted and bow-tied tenors and basses. Higher still the massive pillars, soaring vaults and fabulous round window kept drawing my eye upwards.

I am still at the 'pinching myself' stage, having only moved to live in Orkney recently. 'Am I really sitting here?' I thought. 'Am I really sitting in this beautiful place, listing to this super sound swirling and crashing all around me?' Bev, my wife, was singing with the sopranos. It was her first go at singing anywhere in public, let alone in a cathedral choir. I can't be sure but I think I heard her angelic voice drifting down to me where I sat, proudly, in the front row. Then again it may just have been a regular angel sitting somewhere up in the triforium or clerestory.

It had been my idea to live in Orkney. Bev had been very busy with other projects in the south so I know she gave up a lot to come north, and I know she worried she would not be fully occupied. I feel a huge responsibility for her happiness here. The choir only took up one evening a week to rehearse, and then one Sunday to perform, but it represented a new challenge and a new achievement. We didn't come here simply intending to replicate our old lives, with a new view from the window, we came for a new life. The choir, and other things, are certainly part of that.

Storm Caroline blew in one December night. Dog woke me at 7.00am to go outside so I pulled the Helly Hansen over my dressing gown. Just outside was fairly sheltered but beyond the corner of the house I was almost blown off my feet. My glasses were blown off my face and then, of course, I couldn't see to look for them. Fetching a spare pair from the house, holding them on with one hand and torch in the other, I soon found the first pair, about ten feet across the lawn – undamaged. Motorists passing on their early morning commute must have enjoyed telling the story at coffee break: 'That guy at the new hoose was oot in the gale, wi' his dressing gown blowin' up roond his waist.' They're entitled to smile.

When my shed was piled in sections waiting to be erected, during an earlier gale, I was out in the dark again (yes, dressing gown and Helly Hansen), arranging heavy timbers to prevent it blowing away. Bright headlights pierced the gloom and a huge tractor with a scoop full of breeze blocks trundled down the drive. It was Ivan, a neighbour from the hill opposite who had seen my plight (and more besides I shouldn't be surprised).

'I thought you might be needing these,' he said.

I hadn't met Ivan before but he and I worked together to arrange the blocks round the shed panels and then went inside for tea and a blether. Ivan wasn't being heroic but I will always remember his help that morning whenever I think of him from now on. Incidentally, I wonder if that's why they're called breeze blocks.

Whenever one moves to a new community, one has to pick up on local etiquette fairly quickly. Our first strong wind arrived on a Friday – dustbin day in Orphir. I was unprepared. The bin and its contents would surely be scattered. I could see the amber flashing lights of the bin lorry back up the village so, thinking quickly, I reversed my van to the kerb and secured the bin to the door handles using a bungee. The bungee would give a quick release and not slow the men, I thought. Sadly, they left it unemptied.

I phoned the council to see what I'd done wrong.

'It was the bungee,' the lady said. 'Dustbin etiquette forbids them.'

Between gales, I built a sturdy rail with galvanised chain and hooks. Even Storm Caroline couldn't prevent our bin collection that day.

CHAPTER EIGHTEEN

# Orcadians

DURING A CHRISTMAS episode of *Celebrity Mastermind*, John Humphries asked the question, 'An Orcadian is a native, or inhabitant, of which islands?' The contestant didn't know but the answer given was 'the Orkneys'. I know there are those who will say one can't be truly an Orcadian unless born here – and it's 'Orkney', not 'the Orkneys' – but we are committed to a life here now and wouldn't object to anyone calling us Orcadians.

I am a Yorkshireman but can I be an Orcadian too? I guess not, but it was a nice idea while it lasted. After all, I was born near Hull so am qualified, by birth, to play cricket for Yorkshire – one can't have everything. Nevertheless, there are a lot of incomers who have been here a long time and have made major contributions to Orkney life. They have helped make Orkney a thriving, vibrant, attractive (best in the UK) place to live. A neighbour was telling me recently that Orkney is very different from the Orkney of his childhood – largely due to the huge influx of 'new islanders' bringing new ways and ideas to the county. He didn't say whether he thought this was for the better or the worse. A bit of both I suspect.

Sir Peter Maxwell Davies came here from the south and left an enormous legacy. A firm friendship with the native writer George Mackay Brown gave Orkney, and the world, the wonderfully enduring St Magnus Festival. St Magnus himself was born here, incidentally, in 1080. Another Orcadian, John Rae, was born in Orphir and through almost superhuman travails showed us the way through the Northwest Passage.[1]

Domenico Chiocchetti came from Italy but was brought to Orkney as a prisoner of war. He was billeted in a hut on the tiny

---

1 Climate change might lead us to wish we didn't have such an easy route today.

island of Lamb Holm and set to work during the day building causeways between islands. In their spare time, Domenico and friends built the most beautiful Italian Chapel from scrap. When released at the end of the war, he stayed to finish it and then came back in the 1960s to carry out restoration work. Not an Orcadian but most definitely a much loved and respected character in the islands' history.

Maria Sutherland survived the war in Europe by the skin of her teeth. As she opened the front door to step outside, a bomb fragment came in and flew straight down the hall and out through the back wall of the house – no one was harmed. Had the shrapnel hit the closed door she may well have been killed. After the war Maria came to Orkney, via London, married Alex Sutherland, an Orkney farmer, and has lived here ever since. Maria's two daughters – Monica and Kathleen – were born here, as were her five grandchildren – Ryan, Natalia, Alan, Linda and Graham. Alan, sadly, passed away far too young but there are now four great grandchildren – Archie and Kerry (twins) plus Jenna and Becky. Most of them are still here in Orkney but Kathleen lives in Spain and Natalia, an archaeologist, goes where the work takes her. The twins were born in an Aberdeen hospital. Graham's wife, Jane, had only gone there for a scan and did not make it back to the islands before their arrival, but woe betide anyone who might suggest they are not Orcadian. The swirl of humanity picks people up and casts them on the world's shores to be of service, hopefully, to whichever community they find themselves in. We're all just part of the human family in the end.

There is one accident of birth that's less important now than in earlier times. The Ba' – a Kirkwall street game played each Christmas and New Year's Day – is contested between the Uppies, born in the south end of the town, and the Doonies from the north. You belong to one camp or the other according to where you were born in, or first entered, the town. (In 1988, I first arrived in Kirkwall along the main road from Stromness, so I'm a Doonie.) These days, however, most Orkney children are born in Uppie territory at the hospital, so Tarik, Ronnie, Thorfinn, Olivia and the others will be allowed to choose sides according to family affiliations.

I was watching otters the other day and got chatting to an Orcadian lady who happened to be there too. 'Well, I hope that, whether your stay will be long or short, you'll be very happy here,' she said. A two-winter visitor? I don't think so.

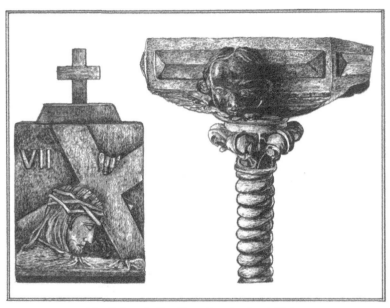

Details from Italian Chapel interior, Lamb Holm.

CHAPTER NINETEEN

# Fifty-nine Degrees
# of Northness

I LOVE ISLANDS. I also love the idea of 'northness', so Orkney suits me just fine.

On a windy Sunday in January, I parked beside the Peedie Sea in Kirkwall. This is a remnant of the actual sea, at the landward side of the harbour that was enclosed when a road and sea wall was built. Part of it has been encircled by manicured lawns and footpaths to create a model boating lake. A pensioner was remotely controlling HMS *Ark Royal* through proportionately mountainous seas.

The waves on the Peedie Sea are always worst at the downwind side. The low, encircling parapet affords some shelter and that is where I found the ducks. There were mallard, goldeneye, long-tailed and wigeon. Ringed plover huddled on the shore and a few gulls were hanging about.

The goldeneye (*Bucephala clangula*[1]) is a fabulous bird. The male in winter – which is when we are most likely to see him in Scotland – has a predominantly white body, a green-glossed black head with a bold white spot behind the base of the dark, triangular bill. It has, as you would expect, a golden eye.

The summer breeding territories of the goldeneye are the lakes and rivers of the forested taiga zone which extends across northern Eurasia and North America. There have been a few breeding reports in Scotland but mainly the birds come here to escape the harsher winters at home, so when I see them on the Peedie Sea, or in the sheltered Orkney bays, I feel a true connection with the far north. I am glad we can offer them sanctuary and so play our part in their eventual breeding success in the summer.

---

1 *Clangula* from the Latin *clangere*, to resound.

The goldeneye's cousin, the long-tailed duck (*Clangula hyema-lis*[2]) also visits us in winter. There were a few on the Peedie Sea and in Swanbister Bay when I looked. Slightly smaller than the golden-eye, the long-tailed duck is beautifully marked with a pinkish bill band, dark cheek patch, white and pale grey body and, of course, a long tail. The whiteness of the bird helps distinguish it from the other duck with a long tail, the pintail. There are a tiny number of breeding records or claims for Britain.

Seeing these birds is a bit like looking over the fence, or through a window, into the true north. One can imagine wolves, bears, Arctic foxes and bison roaming about – just beyond our reach.

We have the northern lights in Orkney too, although I've yet to see them properly. I did see a green smudge once but I live in hope. One shouldn't be too optimistic: the pictures posted on social media and in books are produced by cameras, of course, and they are much more sensitive to the extremes of colour than the human eye. What you see in a photograph will often be better than with the naked eye. It may even have been worth my snap-ping the green smudge – who knows what might have been lurk-ing behind?

Orkney is equidistant from London and Iceland (about 550 miles) and only 300 from Bergen in Norway, even less from Faroe. In Viking times, Orkney was at a truly significant cross-roads in the emerging trade routes between Scandinavia, southern Europe via the North Sea, and Ireland and the west via the Pentland Firth and Cape Wrath. Today, sea traffic still braves the hugely power-ful tidal swirls and eddies between Orkney and the north Scottish coast. Only a couple of years ago, a cruise ship got caught, on a flat calm night, in an eddy so powerful that passengers fell down stairs, the buffet ended up on the floor and officers on the bridge were clinging on for dear life. The ship righted itself in a few moments and there was no lasting harm done. Standing orders aboard such vessels now require all the engines to be started and extra officers be on the bridge when approaching the Pentland Firth.

---

2 *hyemalis*, of winter.

During Orkney winters, there is enough light every day, but only just, to carry on an outdoor life. The darkness is punctuated by the most glorious of sunrises and sunsets. No sooner has one ended than the other one starts. Whenever we see the sun in December or January, it seems to be rising or setting. It sets a challenge for the postman, the farmer and the builder but for us dog-walkers and birdwatchers it just requires a bit of organisation. I don't have to feel guilty about sitting in my chair as night falls over Scapa Flow at three in the afternoon. It feels *north* and *other* and *special* and I think about the Neolithic folk in their houses at Skara Brae, closing the flaps and gathering round the fire, safe and secure for the night. I think they will have loved it too.

Eider ducks – by permission of Tim Wootton.

CHAPTER TWENTY

# Sailing Home

ABOUT TWICE A year I travel to speak about Scottish islands on cruise ships. I never tire of sharing Shetland, the Outer Hebrides, Mull – or Orkney – with folk who might be seeing them for the first time.

I arrived back from a trip to Faroe in October, via Shetland, calling into Kirkwall for the day on the way to Tilbury. I was up early, drinking coffee in the breakfast room, as we sailed down the east side of Orkney into Hatston. It was dark but I saw first North Ronaldsay lighthouse, then Start Point on Sanday and the light on Auskerry before, finally, all the winking buoys, pier lights and streetlights of Kirkwall. I was sailing home. As a 'new islander', the sensation of coming home by sea is still quite new, having been used to nothing more romantic than motorway signs to tell me if I'm nearly there yet. It occurred to me that travellers from these islands must always have been deeply moved by their first sight of land on the way home.

At the end of the 1960 film *Sink the Bismarck!*, Michael Hordern, playing the part of Admiral Sir John Tovey on board HMS *King George V*, once the battle was over gave the order 'Yeoman, make to the Admiralty, Bismarck is sunk, we are returning to Scapa Flow'. The relief was then acted out on all the faces around him. In the film, it was acted but that really happened (in 1941) and we can only imagine the actual relief felt by everyone on board when Duncansby and Pentland Skerries lights (switched on briefly for them) were spotted. The swell they had been feeling for days would suddenly drop on passing Stroma and Swona, a password was given to allow safe passage under the guns at Hoxa and Flotta. They would proceed to their allocated anchorage in the Flow and hear the chain rattle out, engine stop and then silence. The same would have been felt by Admiral Jellicoe's men on returning from the Battle of Jutland in 1916. Ships and men had been lost, so the relief cannot have been too sweet, but very welcome nevertheless.

Orkney was a staging post for ships sailing to and from the northwest during the 18th and 19th centuries. Explorers, whalers and fishing boats often called in for fresh water, supplies and recruits. Sir John Franklin's ill-fated expedition sailed from Stromness, as did one of his would-be rescuers, Orkney's very own Dr John Rae. Franklin sailed up the east coast of England and Scotland, from his starting point in the Thames, and made landfall in Stromness, Orkney. Michael Palin's account of Franklin's flagship – *Erebus* – gives the following excerpt from a letter by Lieutenant Fairholme:

> I never saw anything more lovely than the scene last night, as we ran through the narrow passages among these little islands. In themselves there is nothing of the beautiful, as they are perfectly bare, but there was such a sky and such a summit on such a glass-like sea that it was quite worthy of the Gulf of Smyrna.

The Hudson's Bay Company had a big presence in Stromness too. Their ships would have had little to guide them home across the Atlantic. They could measure latitude and longitude – if they could see the sun – but right in their path lay Sule Skerry with associated stacks and reefs. The massive cliffs of Cape Wrath on the northwest corner of Scotland provided a landfall from which to correct their bearing home to Hoy Sound and the harbour entrance but, once again, only if visibility was good enough. By the 1880s, HBC had moved into a department store operation, with shops in what would become Canada's major cities. The need for British manufactured goods was great. Steam, as well as sailing ships were hurrying to and fro. A lighthouse was established on Cape Wrath in 1828, on Sule Skerry in 1895 and three years later on Noup Head on the island of Westray. These must have come as a huge boon to navigators and watchers from crows' nests when approaching Orkney. So many boats were lost on Sule Skerry and associated rocks that fishermen went there specifically to salvage what they could. Even after the light was established, there continued to be losses right up to 1968.

For the purposes of this story, I had hoped to find that Captain Cook returned from one or other of his voyages via Stromness but it was not to be. Cook was murdered in the Hawaiian Islands, in 1779, after a dispute over the theft of a boat by the locals. His ships, *Resolution* and *Discovery*, however, did arrive in Stromness, having been blown north in a storm on their way home. They tied up in the harbour and men came ashore to collect fresh water from Login's Well in 1780. This before proceeding south down the east coast of Scotland and England. The well was sealed in 1931 but the visit is clearly recorded on the glass cover.

During their short stay in Orkney, the men of *Resolution* and *Discovery* sold some of Captain Cook's artefacts, principally his dinner service, to buy provisions for the final leg of their journey home. A lovely cabinet full of the plates can be viewed in the dining room at Skaill House, alongside the table which is laid for an elegant dinner. It is more than likely Cook's senior officers were entertained there, whilst other ranks explored the ale houses and taverns of Stromness.

In 1845, Sir John Franklin called into Stromness to draw fresh water from Login's Well and dine with notable Orcadians of the time, before setting out across the Atlantic in HMS *Erebus* and HMS *Terror*. Franklin, of course, perished with all his men on this expedition so the cliffs of Hoy would most certainly have been his last view of home. The loss of the Franklin expedition remains the greatest catastrophe in the history of exploration by the Royal Navy.

Arctic explorer and employee of Hudson's Bay Company Dr John Rae was raised at Hall of Clestrain in Orphir, Orkney. His boyhood home still stands – just – and was bought in 2018 by the John Rae Society which intends to restore it and establish a world-class centre for the interpretation of Arctic exploration. At the same time, it will clarify and celebrate the enormous contribution John Rae made to that subject. Rae discovered the final link in the Northwest Passage – subsequently named Rae Strait – to the east of King William Island where no passage had been thought to exist.

Rae reported his findings to the Admiralty in London in 1854 but then came home to Orkney the same year to lick his wounds after being shunned and vilified by much of Victorian society and

establishment, for his report also included the news that Sir John
Franklin's men had resorted to cannibalism in the last resort to try
to save themselves. Much of Rae's evidence came from his close
friendship with the Inuit and what they told him. He landed in
Kirkwall after sailing from London. The story goes that, upset and
furious at the non-arrival of a carriage he had ordered, he stormed
off and walked the 14 miles home.

In 2014, the latest in a long line of expeditions finally discovered the remains of Franklin's two ships. *Erebus* was found using
sophisticated 21st century sonar buoys. She lies, not too deep,
to the west of King William Island, still remarkably intact for a
wooden sailing vessel that has lain on the seabed for over 160
years. The full outline and shape are clear. On the first dive, can-
ons and the ship's bell were found. Ownership of the wrecks (HMS
*Terror* has also been found) has been passed to the Canadian Government but who would bet against a touring exhibition of finds
arriving at the British Museum, Greenwich Observatory or even
Stromness Museum sometime? Franklin did not make it home but
the remains of his expedition may yet sail in through Hoy Sound
or past Hoxa Head into Hamnavoe – the Haven Bay.

The author on board his boat – *Fulmar* – in Stromness marina.

CHAPTER TWENTY-ONE

# The Longest Night

ORKNEY IS FAMOUS for being wet, cold, bleak, barren... and dark in the winter. There's nothing to do, people imagine, apart from huddle round the peat fire, with the straw cowl on your Orkney chair protecting you from the draught whistling under the croft house door. The worst time, of course, must be the winter solstice. This is the shortest day, bringing with it the longest night – a time for hibernation.

The solstice is a magical time, however. It is acted out in deep space like a dance between Sun and Earth – a celestial pasodoble. At the climax, the Earth reaches a point in its annual orbit when the Northern Hemisphere points more directly away from the Sun than at any other time. In 2018, this happened at 10.22pm on 21 December – towards the deepest part of the longest night. The days on either side are little different.

I went to the cinema in the morning. An odd time, I know, but films don't have very long runs here and, in any case, the timing fitted in well with five-a-side walking football afterwards, in the sports hall next door.

Later we took a walk, Dog and I, along the cliffs at Orphir. It was 2.30pm and already the light was taking on that dusken quality unique to late December. An hour before dark at any other time is different, it's almost as though the sky knows something we don't. Artists and photographers are abroad. The air and sea were totally still. The loudest sounds came from the fulmars cackling on the ledges. I first heard this noise 40 years ago, on a Hebridean pebble beach, in a cove between two vertical cliffs. The echo in the stillness amplified the primordial sound and I think of that day every time I hear it.

Goldeneye, merganser, mallard, eider and wigeon drifted with their mates, waiting for a light cue in January that will trigger mating in earnest. The strengthening sun will penetrate their brains, cue in the hormonal orchestra and direct the reproductive performance. Already they suspect a change is coming so dare not let mates out of their sights. Four whooper swans visiting from the north flew overhead in line astern. I snapped them and the print shows wings alternately up and horizontal in perfect symmetry from front to back. Their rise and fall was perfect – an aerial waltz perhaps. Duncansby Head (20 miles away) and the Scarabens (mountains in Caithness 50 miles away) were visible on the Scottish mainland through the clear air.

On our way back to the house, it was already civic twilight – the horizon was still visible and objects could still be made out. The Orkney Islands Council provided our village streetlights with Christmas illuminations again this year and I am pleased we had our old friend the red snowflake on our post. When new friends were due, it was handy being able to say, 'Look for the red snowflake.' Along the street, there were skiing Santas, snowmen and reindeer in blue, green and yellow.

Just time to shower and change before hurrying down to St Magnus Cathedral for the evening performance of Rutter's *Magnificat* given by The Winter Choir and Orkney Camerata in aid of Malawian children in need. The cathedral sound is fabulous but the 12th century planners did not anticipate 21st century audiences. If you want a good seat you must get there early, so I queued in the cold with other enthusiasts and, when the doors opened, secured a spot on the third row. The concert-goer first in line said, 'I need to be close enough to see the cellist's shoes.' She declared herself happy in this regard when we spoke at the interval.

By now it had passed civic twilight, nautical twilight, even astronomical twilight and was proper dark. Light from the town's Christmas lights made viewing of the Milky Way and northern lights impossible when the cathedral turned out. We had to wait until the road across Hobbister Moor for those treats.

Next day there were just a few flocks of lapwing, curlew and greylag geese flapping by, competing for the prize for best Charleston I thought, so still not much going on.

Fulmars.

CHAPTER TWENTY-TWO

# Wreath

WALKING ON SCAPA Beach is a most therapeutic, thought-provoking activity. Dog is content with her ball and the very act of walking is relaxing. Add to this the wind, sound of the sea, the birds and, more often than you might think, the sunshine.

On 3 November 2018, I found a poppy wreath tucked up under the cliff by Scapa Distillery. It had been three weeks since the HMS *Royal Oak* memorial service out in the bay and I could scarce believe it had been in the sea that long, so fresh was its condition.

The label was only just decipherable, however, but I made out:

Leading Seaman

Ronald Derbyshire

PJ/X 125355

Always Remembered.

A look at the crew list confirmed Ronald had died on *Royal Oak*. He had been 29. I asked around and discovered the wreath had been laid over the wreck by Ronald's grandson Gareth, who is current Chair of the Royal Oak Association. I re-laid the wreath at the memorial garden.

Gareth told me Ronald had left a two-year-old son (Gareth's father) also called Ronald, who passed away in 2001. Gareth (actually Ronald Gareth) was born in October 1969, just 30 years after the death of his grandad. His father had always made sure Gareth knew the story of his grandad which is why he feels such a responsibility to his memory, and the memory of all his grandad's shipmates. One of Gareth's grandsons is also Ronald.

Picking up the wreath on Scapa and speaking to Gareth, I have made a connection with a named person from *Royal Oak* – no longer will I think only of that terrible number of 834. The other

833 all had families too, one way or another. I hope they are all alive, somewhere, in someone's memory.

A week later, I was back on the beach in the most glorious sunny, calm weather for Armistice Day, 100 years after the end of WWI. Danny Boyle had inspired *Pages of the Sea* – a sand art commemoration of service men and women who fell in that conflict.

About 2,000 Orkney folk gathered on the beach and along the wall to watch the etching in sand of a 20m square image of the face of Lieutenant Robert Taylor MC from Flotta. Robert, the only son of Robert and Jane Taylor (neé Sutherland) died aged 24 in 1917 after being wounded at Poelcappelle. He had been awarded the Military Cross at Passchendaele for: 'A rare exhibition of tenacity and skill in sending back information of the highest value'. 'He was,' said his commanding officer, 'a highly popular and efficient young officer who had been through two years of the hardest fighting.' Lieutenant Taylor is buried in Belgium. His MC is in the Orkney Museum in Kirkwall.

The 2018 Armistice Day has certainly been high profile, much more so than, say, the 2017 event, but we would expect that. We take particular note of round figures in the way we remember history. 2017 was 900 years after the murder of Earl Magnus; 2016 was 100 years after the Battle of Jutland and the loss of HMS *Hampshire*. In 2019, it was 50 years passed since the men of Longhope lifeboat, TGB, were lost.

We must be careful not to glorify war, of course, but when I stood outside the cathedral in the cold one night, watching the moving images projected onto the cathedral façade, everyone was silent. You could, more or less, have heard a pin drop at Scapa, too. I don't think there was much glorifying going on.

We are far less reticent nowadays. We are prepared to make more imaginative and public shows when we mark events. The taciturn stiff upper lip has given way to the thoughtful, proud and grateful thanks for services rendered and sacrifices made. I suppose there might have been some ceremony surrounding the 50th Armistice Day (when I was 17) but I don't remember any.

There would have been a cub and scout parade no doubt 'for Remembrance Sunday' but as youngsters I think we would have been left to intuit the meaning and draw our own conclusions, if any.

I was struck in 2018 by just how many children and young people *have* been interviewed for their views of events. They are the people, of course, for whom this was the most important. One young man on the news said, 'If *we* don't remember, then who will pass the message on to the next generation?' Who indeed?

Ronald Derbyshire's wreath.

CHAPTER TWENTY-THREE

# Everyone Is Our Neighbour

WE LOUPED[1] OFF the ferry in August 2017. We were strangers; now everyone is our neighbour.

Good neighbours, traditionally, will lend a cup of sugar, without any thought of payment. The favour is always returned in kind, of course, and this is how the world turns in communities like Orkney. You may remember I told you about Ivan, who arrived with a ton of breeze blocks at 6.00am on the morning when Storm Caroline blew in. He had seen the panels of my new shed, piled on the drive waiting to be erected, flapping in the wind and came to secure them.

When I bought a small boat recently in which to go off exploring Scapa Flow, I put a message on Facebook that I needed gear. Within the day, I was invited to three sheds to 'Have a look through and see if there was anything you want'. I paid for some items but came away with armfuls of gifted fenders, ropes, life jackets and a clever device that measures wind speed. Thank you, lads, you know who you are. When the engine wouldn't start, I met John in the street who came to look at it. He phoned Norman who said, 'Bring it round'. It was soon fixed and plans for trips to islands were being made.

In shops, I am getting used to, 'Well, take them both home and see how you go, then keep the one you want and pop in some time to pay for the other.' Often, nothing is written down. 'We're short of change just now, come back and pay in a peedie while.' The classic one was Charlie the postman on our first day: 'Leave your front door unlocked so I can deliver your parcels. If you can't do

---

1 Ferry loupers: people who are not Orcadian and having arrived by ferry. The term is often used a bit negatively and some prefer 'new islander'.

that then leave your bathroom window open – but remember to put your toilet seat down.'

The carpark was full the other day but a man indicated he was leaving so I took his space. Just then my phone rang – Bev, as usual, reminding me of some chore or other. Walking to pay at the machine, I saw the original owner of the space had waited until I finished the call to give me his ticket – which still had almost an hour left on it. (Sorry, OIC, if this is not allowed, but the opportunity to give and receive in this anonymous, neighbourly fashion far outweighs any legal rules.)

One cannot be too precious about one's personal goings-on in Orkney. The nurse at the outpatients turned up sitting next to Bev at choir practice, and the lady dispensing my prescription said, 'Oh, Mr Clubley, hello, you're my new neighbour.'

When I'm writing, I often have to track people down. I start with the local phone book and dial everyone with the appropriate initials. If the wrong person answers, they say, 'Oh, aye, I ken the one you want, it's me brother. His number is 811470, but he's away oot just noo, try the morn.' There is no guardedness, no suspicion that I might be trying to sell something or commit identity theft. I'm sure someone might take advantage of this from time to time, but most people here are open and honest so the approach works just fine.

I met the bird artist in the street one day, carrying a painting home from the framers. He opened the folder and I bought the image of curlews on the spot. Next day I was sunbathing in the garden (yes, that's what I said) when he ran down the side path, leapt over the fence into the field, shouting 'You've a rose coloured starling here – put the kettle on.'

Everybody waves. I wave to coaches full of tourists as they pass my front garden. They wave back and I'm sure they're thinking they'd like to live here, be my neighbours and mow grass overlooking the sea. I certainly remember what it was like when I was on the outside looking in and, beuy, do I owe some sugar?

CHAPTER TWENTY-FOUR

# Theatre Nights

PICTURE THE SCENE: it is February 1602. The curtain has just come down on the first ever public performance of *Twelfth Night* by William Shakespeare at Middle Temple Hall, one of the Inns of Court in London.

In Orkney, like as not, it being February 1602, a gale was raging and the sky was dark. Waves were crashing against the Yesnaby cliffs and plumes of spray were breaking right over the Hole O' Row. Few ventured out. More peat would be placed on the fire and maybe a dried cow pat or a piece of wood from the shore. Tales would be told, poems composed and read. There would be music, song and laughter. No one switched on the television, let alone went out to the cinema.

Even in the brand new Earl's Palace, then under construction in Kirkwall, Earl Patrick Stewart would not have Netflix. He had pages, lackeys and trumpeters clothed in red and yellow, but of DVDs and Blu-ray there were none. The only flat screen in the palace was in front of the fire or to prevent draughts at the door.

In 2018 we sat with fellow 'theatre-goers' in the Phoenix cinema, Kirkwall, to watch a live screening of *Twelfth Night* from the Royal Shakespeare Company's home in Stratford-upon-Avon. The wind still blew, waves still crashed and the night was black and clear. Many stars shone. Stars Adrian Edmondson and Kara Tointon also shone in the cinema as Malvolio and Olivia in Shakespeare's play.

Who'd have thought it? Here we were, drinks and snacks in hand, watching live theatre from 600 miles away. We heard the buzz and applause of the audience in Stratford (we could even have joined in the clapping if self-consciousness hadn't got the better of us). We had an interval when they did – and a short documentary about the costume department.

By the miracle of technology, we have the RSC live, blockbuster movies and global telecommunications to go with our wide open spaces, birds, flowers and clean air. We have everything. And what is more, by the same miracle, the folk down in Stratford can watch Orkney's otters and puffins or view our Neolithic houses.

Speaking of entertainment, Julie Felix came to sing for us. Julie was 80 years old in June 2018 and was working on a new studio album – her first for ten years – with which to celebrate.

They say that if you remember the '60s you weren't really there. Well, I do remember them, and I was there, but I don't think I paid enough attention at the time. The Summer of Love (almost 50 years ago), Flower Power and Ban the Bomb all passed me by in a blur. My room at college had some graffiti, left by a previous student, saying things about Vietnam. I listened to The Byrds sing 'Mr Tambourine Man' and a song about wearing flowers in San Francisco. I even played badminton with Deep Purple (they rehearsed in our community hall). I didn't really get any of it. It was just the stuff happening around me.

Julie Felix got it. She spoke to me after her gig in Stromness Town Hall. She's a bit older than me so I asked if she had realised at the time how significant the 1960s were.

'Yes,' she said. 'It was a special time. I didn't think it would end, or that it would be interpreted so much by future generations. My dad had given me a guitar and I just started singing about what I believed in – rights for the individual and such. I was involved with CND and the Aldermaston March. My first album came out in 1964. Songs like "Blowin' in the Wind" and "We Shall Overcome" were getting into the charts – it was unbelievable.'

Julie became interested in 'Earth Mysteries' during the '80s. Proponents hold certain sites to be sacred. Stonehenge is probably the best known but our own Ring of Brodgar, Maeshowe and Skara Brae are also up there. She believes in the mysticism of these places and the whole idea of Mother Earth. She deplores the damage being done to the Earth by corporate greed.

When we talk to the archaeologists, they don't know for sure what the low, stone walls being unearthed at Ness of Brodgar were intended for. There is all manner of speculation based on hard scientific investigation and measurement. They talk of religious and social ceremonies; government, trade and just about every activity still practised today when people meet. If people like Julie Felix, with all that she has lived through, find mysticism in them, if they represent, for her, Mother Earth and all that's wholesome, then I would not wish to argue.

CHAPTER TWENTY-FIVE

# Sky Blue Pink with Yellow Dots

I DO LIKE to be beside the seaside. In Orkney, one is never far from water, either the salty stuff or a fresh inland loch. I was in Stromness on a warm, sunny day in May, sitting at a pavement café having lunch, when the ferry from Scrabster – MV *Hamnavoe* – blew its horn to alert boaters of its imminent arrival. I could see her upper works against the line of roofs – they were only things moving so I knew what they were. How lovely, I thought, to be sitting here with this great big ship arriving and reminding me of where I live, between the North Sea and the Atlantic Ocean. I looked around for more evidence, as if my fresh Westray crab sandwich wasn't proof enough.

On the pier, two men were painting a wooden fishing boat, lifted from the harbour and perched, above my eyeline, on blocks for the purpose. I could see all the bits usually in the water so the proportions were unfamiliar. I had been watching their progress for a couple of weeks and every time I passed, it reminded me where I was.

Winter in Orkney is a thing used to impress visitors, compare with neighbours and brag about to southern softies. I have done two winters now (two usually qualifies a person as a stayer) and they have been quite mild, although lately I've sensed some nostalgia for really severe winters by older folk who sound as though they want them back. Even so, there is nothing to beat a lovely, calm, sunny (hot?) day in May – anything around 15°C or more, warm and sunny enough for t-shirt and sunglasses, is fine. We get plenty of those days in Orkney. Friends arriving from south during their heat wave step from the plane into our 15°C heat and declare how nice it is to be comfortable.

Along the cliff path, the thrift is forming its pink cushions again. Dandelions are already going to seed and all those little blue and purple flowers are out. The low willow bushes and things with berries later are in leaf. The ditch beside the road is full of water blobs (marsh marigolds). Gold they are, so I climbed in to get a picture, conscious they would be passed all too soon. There are poppies, bluebells, daisies and buttercups. The snowdrops of January seem pale by comparison now.

'Puffins are back,' can be a greeting in the street. 'They've been spotted on Marwick Head, Westray, Burrick and Brough of Birsay.' Bonxies (great skuas) patrol the cliffs whereon fulmars sit, hopeful of a chick. Hares race round the fields in gangs and the curlews' 'bubbling' landing flight goes on all day and night. The oystercatchers complained all winter and continue to protest. Are they never satisfied?

There's a cruise ship in today, a big 'un – 3,000 folk from Canada I think. It was mostly Germans yesterday and will be Japanese tomorrow. My usual seat for coffee has been taken but I don't mind squeezing onto a table to be interrogated: 'Do you live here? Really? You're so lucky. This is our first visit. It's fabulous. We've been all round the island and seen the standing stones and the little chapel. The weather is glorious. Someone on the ship had said it rained and blew gales all the time.'

The spring colours of Orkney are like nowhere else. Blues, greens and whites basically, but *what* blues, greens and whites? The grass (there's a lot of grass) makes chlorophyll again and turns its most verdant colour; the strengthening sun penetrates the sea and lochs and switches on the deep blue lights to shine from below. Across the loch, there's more green and then a band of different blue – the sky – plain or with bright, Daz-white clouds to give your photos a bit of background (hint: use a polarising filter if you have one). When the sun goes in, the colours switch off.

It was open day at our fabulous, new state-of-the-art hospital. I took my shades off to go inside but it was so light and airy I could have kept them on. It is a super investment in the people of Orkney and their futures. All that sea and sun; all those wild things and wide, open spaces, but we can live here too, secure in the knowledge we are safe and cared for.

Come for a week, or a fortnight if you can. You won't be disappointed. Fifty years ago, Neil and Buzz enjoyed two hours on the surface of the moon and declared themselves happy with the grey. You'll go home happy too. There's nowhere like it. Oh, did I mention the turquoise?

CHAPTER TWENTY-SIX

# Taking in the View

AFTER ALMOST TWO years, I still haven't explored the whole of Orkney. I don't know, for instance, if that particular beach is good for Groatie Buckies – small cowrie shells highly prized by Orcadians – or if the view from that hill is particularly fine. I haven't eaten at that restaurant nor have I seen what is round that next corner on my walk.

To friends in the south, Orkney is a tiny, remote Scottish island. They believe one could walk round in a day and then want somewhere else to visit. The truth is that since settling here we have become the same creatures of habit we were in the big city – the same selection of walks, regular eateries, favourite shops and – dare I say it in high summer – same telly programmes.

I post photographs of views on Facebook to impress the southerners but I realised the other day, they are starting to be a bit repetitive: Hoy from Warbeth; Hoy from Clestrain; Orphir from Scorradale; Clestrain from Scorradale; and Scapa Bay from Scapa Beach. I think they might have noticed by now and are confirmed in their view that Orkney's not very big.

I was thinking about this and then realised it doesn't really matter. Of course I tend to see the same views: I live in the same place. Every time I go anywhere it is over Scorradale, Hobbister or Heddle (I forgot to mention the view back from Hobbister to Orphir is my favourite). I love those panoramas, I never tire of them so it's okay. After all, it wouldn't do if love – of anything – didn't last a bit longer than two years.

I once spoke to a 90-year-old lady who had lived on Fair Isle all her life but had never seen the north lighthouse. On an island just three miles long and half a mile wide, that seemed improbable but her nephew confirmed it. She was the eldest of six so stayed home to prepare the food when the others went to the peats (the only reason a Fair Islander would have for going near the lighthouse would have been the peats). I checked the figures and Mainland Orkney has 75 times the area of Fair Isle so that made me feel less of a stay-at-home.

I do enjoy the vistas so I thought I would cogitate what it is about them that is so great. First of all, they are wide open: from my room, I can see Duncansby Head, 20 miles away across the Pentland Firth, and the Scaraben Mountains, 50 miles away in Caithness.

Then there are the colours. When the sun shines, the sea-blue is incomparable. The colour is created by white light from the sun shining through it. The red, green and yellow wavelengths are absorbed and only the blue is reflected into our eyes, so that is the colour we see. In shallow water, the light is reflected from the sand and gives us the turquoise. We see this colour best close to shore and especially when flying over the islands.

Blue, it turns out, is everyone's favourite colour. In repeated surveys all over the world, blue comes top. It soothes the mind, apparently. It is serene and mentally calming. Even the words we have for it are tranquil: azure, cerulean, teal. The artist Yves Klein said in 1961, 'The use of one colour over the whole canvas opens the window to freedom.' Someone added later, 'It is a means of evoking immateriality and boundlessness of one's own particular utopian vision of the world.' Wow, no wonder I enjoy looking at the sea.

If I sit with the road behind me and the expansive view to the fore, there are few distractions. Nothing flashes across the field of view to disturb the train of thought. Movements are slowed by distance from the observer. The passage of boats, birds, tractors and people can be taken in, often without turning the head. I can observe goings-on without taking part in them or being seen myself. I have solitude, there's no matter if I fall asleep (as I often do).

On 16 June, almost the longest day, at about 10.00pm, the whole rim of Scapa Flow – Hoy, with Cava in front, Flotta and South Ronaldsay – was glowing pink. The water was flat and calm and the sky still light. I picked up my binoculars and saw that every detail on the far shores was picked out: Flotta's wartime cinema; the old radio communications centre and storage tank at Lyness; houses (ruined and lived in) cliff edges and grassy slopes; boats and clouds were sailing by. It doesn't matter I haven't seen every view in Orkney – I haven't finished this one yet.

CHAPTER TWENTY-SEVEN

# Who'd have thought it?

ORKNEY IS A riddle wrapped in a mystery inside an enigma. 'Where?' they said, when I told my friends in the south I was moving to Orkney. 'What is there? Where will you get your food? Isn't it perpetual darkness? Doesn't the wind blow all the time?'

If you're familiar with Orkney, you'll have heard all this before. You may even have prepared your own standard riposte, such as, 'Oh it's not that bad' or 'But there's hardly any crime.' It's actually a lot better than that. From my house, halfway between Kirkwall and Stromness on Mainland (Orkney's main island is called Mainland. Orcadians never use 'the mainland' to indicate the main body of the UK – that is referred to as 'south'), I have everything I could possibly want within a 20-minute drive. Remote? Not a bit.

For a kick-off, the short drive will be on an excellent road. There'll be an almost perfect surface and no traffic. No traffic lights, few junctions and only the odd roundabout. I can head west, to Stromness for a NorthLink ferry connection south. I can be in Caithness in 90 minutes. The haddock and chips on board is excellent, as is the breakfast. I enjoy an islander discount on everything. MV *Hamnavoe* is a comfortable ship and the journey is (usually) a pleasure. For extra luxury, I can have a cabin on board overnight to save getting up early for the 6.30am sailing.

I can head east to Kirkwall for a NorthLink ship to Aberdeen or Shetland. Both are overnight so a good sleep in a cabin (steerage class aka 'sleeping pod' is available for budget travel).

A few miles south of the ferry pier is Kirkwall Airport (still within the 20-minute rule). Flights can be had to major Scottish cities and even direct to Manchester in the summer. I can go door-to-door to a friend in Derbyshire in about six hours on a good day. Orphir to Chesterfield between meals (with a snack on the plane).

Outside my self-imposed radius, but nevertheless excellent, is St Margaret's Hope and Pentland Ferries, founded by Andrew Banks OBE. The fast catamaran, MV *Pentalina*, carries cars, lorries and passengers across the Pentland Firth in an hour. The new boat, MV *Alfred*, came into service in 2019 and is bigger, comfier, shinier red and the greenest ferry to come into service in Scotland, based on payload per litre of fuel. Together with NorthLink, there are five or six short sea crossings every day of the year plus the overnighters. Spoiled for choice.

When not travelling, I need to be entertained so it's a good thing we have theatres, cinema, leisure centre, music venues, live sport, bars, restaurants. In the soaring St Magnus Cathedral, one can pray or worship but also listen to fabulous choirs and orchestras that come to Orkney or have been formed here. The Winter Choir and St Magnus Festival Choir are drawn from amateur locals in December and June and move the soul. As the crescendos are reached, I gaze upwards at the pillars and stained glass and remember where I am. A 'stone ship' Jocelyn Rendall called it and it is – on a wave of song. There are good schools and a brand new hospital too.

Early Orcadians gathered limpets to eat but we have our choice of supermarkets and local producers. The quality, flavours and variety are excellent. There's space aplenty, of course, so you can grow your own, perhaps in the deep, dark soil of the Kelliequoy allotments.

If you had been thinking of a holiday or a move to Orkney, and I've put you off with all this talk of bustle, fear not, I haven't told you about the other half yet.

I took the ferry to Graemsay and cycled round it one afternoon, never meeting a living soul. From the house, I walk a two-hour circuit of lanes, beach and cliff and am alone. With a friend, I climbed the highest hill on Mainland and we met no one. On Stronsay, I had the beach to myself and gathered fabulous shells. I don't think they get picked over. On Eday, the door locks were rusted, inoperable from decades of redundancy – and they have a resident snowy owl. I passed a basking shark in my boat the other day. The grass and wildflowers grow so tall on the cliff path they arch over and soak my trousers as I swish through. Heather forms a background in the season.

Our winter visitors come from the north; they come for a gentler winter. There are geese and wading birds of several kinds. The puffins go back to sea for the winter but they'll be back in the spring. In the depths of winter, a terrible four-gigawatt current swirls in the Pentland Firth and waves crash at the Yesnaby cliffs, but we are safe and cosy in our island fastness.

CHAPTER TWENTY-EIGHT

# Island Jobs

YOU MAY HAVE seen Sarah Moore on the telly. Sarah came to Orkney, from Edinburgh, in search of a new life. She rented a small house in North Ronaldsay where she lives with her cat, Tiny. Sarah's first job was as a home carer, to which she added: airport firefighter, baggage handler, clerk to the community council, postie, shepherd and lighthouse guide. Sarah has applied to be a dock worker.

People traditionally need several jobs on small islands, there often not being sufficient in one to fill a wage packet. Sarah delights in her jobs, where simply changing from one uniform to another keeps her on the go. North Ronaldsay (population around 50) needs people like Sarah to breathe new life. Together the islanders are working to provide new houses, create new jobs and attract new people. Since the TV programme *The Island That Saved My Life*, there have been 18 expressions of interest in moving to North Ronaldsay – some from much needed young families who would support the school.

We've lived in Orkney two years now and doesn't time fly? Bob Budge handed over the keys on 1 September 2017. Bob was lovely and has built us a solid house. He was right, of course, about us needing to sit in our underpants if we had had an additional stove. He had been right about every other aspect of the job. I never had conversations with him that began with, 'That's going to cost a bit more...' or 'There's been a delay in the supply of...' or 'The plumber has gone off sick so...' Once he started working, his men didn't stop and the keys were handed over on the day he said they would be. The contract we had with him was based on a word and a handshake – it proved to be all that was needed. Bob passed away, aged just 61, in July 2019 but I will always remember the privilege of doing business with him. On a fortnight's holiday, one does not get to know people enough to miss them when they're gone.

We had some concern, before we arrived, that there may not be enough to fill our days. Both officially retired, there was some risk we would not find a holiday idyll a good place to live. When the visitors leave in the autumn, the beaches are windswept and not everywhere is open, would it be so appealing? 'Your problem will be fitting it all in,' said almost everyone, and so it proved. After a few months Bev worried she had taken on too much.

I had met Julia in her Stromness waterfront Bistro when I'd been in for morning coffee, lunch, afternoon tea and just about any other excuse during the months of writing my Orkney book a couple of years before and so as we stepped off the ferry, suitcases in hand, to begin our new life, it was natural to head in for refreshment. An hour later, Bev had made her first commitment – she was to be a waitress three days a week for Julia. By the end of her first shift, her feet ached, her head was spinning and muscles she'd forgotten she had were screaming for her to stop – but still the toilets were to be cleaned, and the floor. Two years later, Bev is still there, now the old head who guides the youngsters. Pacing has been learned, and the names of locals, as well as their regular drinks.

Bev had played the violin in an earlier life, 35 years earlier in fact, and soon discovered the instrument (called a fiddle in Orkney) made a very nice sound in the hands of Jenny Wrigley and others we heard at The Reel. Her very kind husband bought her a student instrument and she commenced weekly lessons with Erica Shearer at Jenny's school. Gradually, a sound appeared, then a note, then several notes in a row (in the right order and with fewer slips) – and, eventually, a tune. We had some friends fae sooth visiting and he nudged and nudged one night until Bev did what she had been itching to do for weeks – she sat at the back of The Strathspey and Reel Society practice and took up her bow. Many of the tunes were too fast but she thrilled at the ones she could do. The routine on Thursdays is that every player is given a tune choice so Bev goes prepared for when the leader says, 'At the back?' He knows her name now but she still sits, and is referred to as 'At the back'. There has been a concert appearance too, and Fiddlers' Rally.

Fiddle practice alternates with running (5K – sometimes longer) and the endorphins released by both are a great boon when gales threaten the shed, planes carrying visitors are delayed or we run out of milk and it's seven miles to the shop.

We had been to Nine Lessons and Carols at Durham Cathedral a few years earlier and Bev enjoyed singing with the congregation. 'There's a thing called The Winter Choir at the cathedral,' she said. 'Anyone can join and they start rehearsing next week for a concert at Christmas.' We hadn't hung all our curtains by this point, nor emptied the boxes, nor erected the shed but off she went to join and came home a soprano. Who knew? St Magnus Festival Choir followed in the spring, led by Paul Rendall, whom we had met when he came to fit our carpet (Orkney society is like that).

Bev is involved with the Orkney College Management Council now so has regained a bit of that professional life she missed since our move. In what little time is left, she helps at the Clan charity shop, takes bookings for the community hall and changes the beds at our B&B.

It was me that campaigned for the move and Bev gave up an awful lot to come with me. I think she has found a good new life. She certainly sleeps well.

## CHAPTER TWENTY-NINE

# Keeping Busy

I FELT AT home in Orkney from the moment I stepped off the ferry. I don't miss anything from my old life, although it was a good one, and there is nothing missing from here that I wish I had.

We built the house with two en-suite B&B rooms and a lounge for guests so, from May to September I get up early to cook full Orcadian breakfasts using only the best local produce. Bev serves at table and does room changes but if she is committed elsewhere on one of her (several) other activities then more falls to me.

By the time tables are cleared, washing up done, Dog walked and sheets put on to wash, it can be time for lunch and a nap. I would feel too guilty going to bed so I stretch out on the dog shelf with a cushion and Dog. Afterwards there's grass to cut if it's dry (we have grass in Orkney, not lawns).

I go to town most days for supplies and usually manage a posh coffee somewhere. If someone ever stole my wallet (unlikely here), the coffee loyalty cards would be worth more in free beverages than the cash. For many Orcadians, a trip to town is not a treat but I still have urban blood that draws me to it. Don't get me wrong, I love the peace out in Orphir. Best of both worlds, I call it.

I was a science teacher for most of my life before retirement but always preferred, as a student, writing an essay to doing a practical. Free at last from the classroom, I have turned to writing as a hobby. Three books on Scottish islands so far and increasingly busy contributions to *Living Orkney* and www.Orkney.com.

I have the Scottish island bug for which there is no known cure. Medical people call it nesomania. My parents took me to Arran, aged about eight in the 1950s, and I was entranced by the idea of a world across and surrounded by water. We had to take a ship – with a café, shop and engines that could be viewed. The island was a new world where things were different. That was truer then than now. Islands are still different, of course, but have communications and services that were lacking 50 years ago.

As a young adult, I discovered Mull, Iona and Staffa – doses of the drug too hard to resist. Addiction was assured. Shetland followed in 1985 and Orkney in 1988 with others such as Eigg, Rum and Gigha along the way, plus many returns to Mull.

The first book, *Scotland's Islands: A Special Kind of Freedom*, was written largely as recollections of about 36 of those early islands. *Orkney: A Special Place* appeared in 2017 after seven months here talking to anyone who would give me time, tea and home-bakes. I almost gave up at the first hearth when someone said, 'You'll never understand Orkney unless you had two Orcadian grandmothers.' I pondered this and, several sessions of tea and buns later, realised my two East Yorkshire grandmothers would have understood their northern counterparts very well. And why not? The two counties are rural, coastal, agricultural, low-lying and out of the mainstream for much of history. Were county twinning ever to be introduced then you could do a lot worse than Orkney and East Yorkshire. I even had a lot of northerly, easterly and north-easterly winds at my childhood bedroom window. One of my East Yorkshire grandmothers used to say, 'Withernsea is a healthy place, the wind blows all the germs away.'

Childhood impressions are indelible. My clockwork lifeboat was out on a shout in Peasholm Park, Scarborough, one day when a lady passer-by said, 'That's not going very fast for a lifeboat.' I have felt protective towards lifeboats and loved them ever since. I grew up watching the slipway launched boat at Spurn Head. Colin Mowat, coxswain of our Stromness lifeboat, told me he caught the bug riding down the slipway from the old red shed (now Scapa Scuba) in the town. This was a treat offered to the children in Shopping Week until Health and Safety brought it to an end. Now, in one of the greatest privileges of my life, I am press officer for RNLI Stromness.

Bev, Dog and I moved to Orkney in 2017. Lifeboats, islands, infinite space, inspiration and frothy coffee. What's not to like?

# Part Two – The Orkney Way of Life on the Outer Islands

IN PART TWO I am looking beyond home in Orphir Village and our new life in Orkney and exploring further afield. In *Orkney – A Special Place*, I spent a lot of time on Mainland. I make no apology for that – there is a lot to see and learn and a lot of people to meet. The inspiration for all my books has been a fascination by, and love of Scottish islands and every aspect of what goes on there, so this time I went to have a look at some of the Orkney islands less visited. Flotta, Stronsay, Papay, Hoy, Eday and Sanday are all inhabited. No one lives on Lamb Holm but a few commute there each day to work. Faray has been uninhabited since 1947 but the farmer still crosses from Eday to tend his sheep.

CHAPTER THIRTY

# Lamb Holm – Treasure Island

JOHN GOW WAS hung for piracy, at Execution Dock, London, in 1725. He was never a very successful pirate. You might say he was hung for a lamb, not a sheep, in that he didn't manage to steal much. Gow grew up in Stromness, Orkney, before running away to sea. He led a mutiny on *The Caroline* in 1724, renaming it *The Revenge* – a pirate ship. After a few unrewarding attacks on Atlantic shipping, he sailed into his home port of Stromness and was warmly received by folk, unaware of his true character (the ship now being called *The George*). The pirates attacked a house at Clestrain (belonging to the Honeyman family at the time but later the site of Hall of Clestrain, home of Arctic explorer

Dr John Rae). They made off to sea but ran aground on Calf of Eday, opposite Carrick House, which they had been planning to rob. Ironically, an old school friend of Gow, James Fea, lived there and he orchestrated the pirates' arrest.

There is an endless fascination with pirates and one thing we think we know about them is they drank a lot of rum (rum originated in the Caribbean during the 17th century, when there were certainly plenty of pirates about).

Collin van Schayk grew up eating liquorice root in Holland but moved with his family to live in Scotland when he was a boy. His dad, Emile van Schayk, started the Orkney Wine Company, operating out of a double garage at first. Orkney wine is made from locally grown fruit such as raspberries, rhubarb, elderflower and blackcurrant. The Orkney red holds its own well against the traditional grape wines.

After periods of working for the Orkney Wine Company and a few years in Edinburgh, Collin came home to Orkney. There had been talk of working for dad again but, like sons the world over, Collin had thoughts of branching out on his own. By this time the wine company had moved to larger, more suitable premises on Lamb Holm, one of Orkney's tiniest islands. The opportunity was too good to miss and Collin took over half the new premises for the rum distillery. J Gow spiced rum was born and the first bottles went on sale in October 2017.

Apart from the winery and distillery, there are other treasures, out of all proportion to its tiny, 100-acre size on Lamb Holm. It has a private airfield, the two runways of which run almost its length and breadth. Island owner Tommy Sinclair, a light aeroplane enthusiast, told me, 'The island looks like a hot-cross bun from the air.'

Lamb Holm is uninhabited today but during WWII, Italian prisoners lived in a small camp of which a few concrete foundations and one stunning chapel remain. At the outbreak of war, Scapa Flow, the large natural harbour enclosed by Orkney's southern islands, was being used as the base for the British Home Fleet, even though there were concerns at the highest level about its security from enemy attack. Concerns so great, in fact, that

The Italian Chapel, Lamb Holm.

most ships were dispersed to the UK west coast, away from the German U-boats. HMS *Royal Oak*, however, remained in Scapa Flow to provide anti-aircraft cover for a radar station just round the corner from Lamb Holm. In September 1939, a German submarine navigated under cover of darkness around the north side of Lamb Holm and into Scapa Flow. She sank *Royal Oak* with torpedoes then escaped the way she had come.

Winston Churchill was furious and ordered immediate construction of barriers to link all the islands in the southern Orkney chain: Mainland to Lamb Holm then on to Glims Holm, Burray and South Ronaldsay. The Italian prisoners were pressed into service for the work (deemed civil rather than military by the addition of a road across the top – thus circumventing the Geneva Convention which prohibits military work by POWs).

Relations between prisoners and captors seem to have been reasonable enough. The Italians were given two disused Nissen huts and other scrap materials from which they fashioned a beautiful little chapel. The Italian Chapel, as it became known, has been cherished on behalf of the Italian men and their families by the people of Orkney to this day. It is famous throughout the world and thousands of visitors come every year to see it. One of the total absurdities of war is that, when it ended, and the men were free to go home, Domenico Chiocchetti chose to stay in Orkney to finish the chapel.

After the war, contractors moved in to demolish the camp. They didn't have the heart to bulldoze the chapel so simply walked away and left it. The landowner – Patrick Graeme – had a daughter, Alison, however, and she would walk across the new causeway in the evenings and fell in love with the peedie chapel. Others began to leave money in the font, which Alison collected and opened a bank account. When the chapel needed a new door, she approached a builder and the work was done (no bill was ever sent). A preservation society was formed and today the Italian Chapel is one of Scotland's greatest treasures – a testament to what can be achieved when love triumphs over hate.

Collin van Schayk drives to work across Churchill Barrier Number One from the village of St Mary's on Mainland, just across the water. Joining the airfield, the chapel and a few sheep is the Orkney Wine Company premises and those of J Gow Rum. It could well be the smallest rum producing island in the world – inspired by pirates, distilled beside the sea. The whole process, once the molasses has been imported from certified suppliers' mills and refineries round the globe, happens on Lamb Holm. Even two (the secret two) of the seven spices in J Gow rum are grown in Orkney. They complement the other five viz vanilla, orange peel, allspice, cassia bark and liquorice. Bottling is also done on Lamb Holm – by hand. 'We did about 1,500 bottles in three hours recently. There were three of us and it was a tough session,' said Collin. He is used to tough days. I met him at the distillery one morning at 10.00am after he had already been hard at it for five hours. 'The still does most of the actual work,' Collin pointed out, 'but I have to be here, constantly checking to make sure it's following the recipe.'

Finally, as if a distillery, winery, airfield, wartime chapel and sheep weren't enough, Lamb Holm boasts a shellfish hatchery – and since nothing is ever allowed to go to waste here, the hatchery is in a flooded quarry that once provided stone for construction of the Churchill Barriers. Treasure doesn't always have to be pieces of eight.

## Historical Footnote:

A contemporary of John Gow was Daniel Defoe, author of possibly the most famous island story – Robinson Crusoe. Defoe also wrote the definitive account of the pirate's life and exploits – what we might call today an in-depth news analysis. In a further footnote, James Fea received the considerable sum of nearly £2,000 for his part in Gow's downfall. His countrymen, however, hounded him through the courts for a share. Fea was ruined and, later, threw in his lot with Bonnie Prince Charlie and the Jacobites. In a final ignominy, his house on Eday was burned by Hanoverians. Another of Gow's time was Rob Roy MacGregor (1671–1734). Is there no end to Scottish history? Just when you think you've got it pinned down, another thread starts to unravel.

J Gow rum, Lamb Holm.

CHAPTER THIRTY-ONE

# Flotta

DAVID SINCLAIR PASSED away in 2019. David lived his entire life on Flotta and was 'Mr Flotta'. His book *Tomorrow is a Whole New Day* was published by the Orcadian Press (2015) and tells the whole story of the island. In 2018, David and I worked together to contribute a fuller version of this story for inclusion in *Reel to Rattling Reel: Memories of Cinema Going* (Cranachan Publishing, 2018). He is missed.

This being Orkney, the name 'Flotta' has an Old Norse derivation: flott-øy, meaning flat, grassy island, distinguishing it from its neighbour, Hoy (há-øy, meaning high island). There are about 2,000 acres of Flotta, rising to around 200 feet.

Flotta is a quiet, rural spot, out of the fast lane for most of history, but three times during the 20th century it was called upon to play a major role in national affairs. In 1914 and 1939, it became a naval base for the British fleet anchored in Scapa Flow. Ships went out from here to fight the Battle of Jutland in 1916, and then again to attack and sink the German battleship, *Bismarck*, in 1941. In 1974, the Occidental Group started construction of an oil terminal to receive oil from the Piper and Claymore fields in the North Sea.

The island has a population of about 60 today but during David Sinclair's childhood, there were around 200 folk. In 1939, the school roll was boosted by children of service personnel based on the island. There were about 40 in the school, so David was never short of pals or mischief to get into. At the peak of hostilities, there were 40,000 military folk in Orkney, all associated with the comings and goings of the fleet and swelling the islands' population by about three times. There were sailors, of course, plus anti-aircraft crews on shore, radar, searchlight, barrage balloon operators, catering and supply people and medics. There was everything needed to keep this huge fighting force supplied, equipped, defended – and entertained.

Mindful of the need to maintain morale, the authorities built squash courts, a gymnasium, dance hall and two NAAFIs on Flotta. Several canteens sold beer, while non-alcoholic beverages were available in the two Church of Scotland huts.

They also provided a brick-built cinema to replace the island's old wooden one. It seated 1,236, including 200 in the grand raked balcony. It had a fitted stage for live drama and music perfor-mances and, when opened in July 1943 by Admiral Sir Bruce Fraser, it had state of the art theatre lighting. Arthur Askey and Jack Hylton both performed at the opening event. Later, Gracie Fields, Yehudi Menuhin and George Formby came to entertain the troops. Someone told me recently that her mum had worked in the NAAFI at Flotta and remembers George Formby having to run off after each number and swap his ukulele for a retuned one, such were the fluctuating atmospheric conditions. Tommy Hand-ley's popular radio show *It's That Man Again* was recorded here. The cinema was always packed, mostly with ships' companies given leave to jump on a liberty boat and come ashore.

David was eight when the cinema opened and well remembers the excitement of watching films there. 'We had no television, only the most basic of radio sets. I recall being smuggled into some screenings by the men who often took pity on us island children. Whether the "smuggling" was to avoid payment I cannot bring to mind. I do remember watching *The Seventh Cross* with Spencer Tracy. I watched through my fingers mostly. It frightened me, even though I had stood with my family as bombs dropped near our quiet, rural island home so was no stranger to fear.'

The cinema was a magnificent, sturdy construction. Three walls, including the foyer and projection room, are still standing in 2019, although the latter has a tree growing through the top. The auditorium roof of corrugated asbestos sheets was sold to a Kirkwall garage years ago. The end wall, supporting the screen, was knocked down to provide a storage space for building mate-rials during the construction of the Oil Terminal.

The cinema was built to last. They had no idea, in 1943, how much longer the war was going to drag on, or how long after that Scapa Flow would be needed as a fleet base. In the event it was boarded up sometime in the 1950s, never to be used again. In later childhood, David and his pals had further adventures climbing in through vents, windows or any way they could find. 'Each time we broke in the authorities boarded up the hole but we always found another. Some involved climbing drainpipes. In this way, the cinema continued to provide excitement and adventure, long after Spencer Tracy had left.'

Earlier this year, by kind permission of current owners, Repsol Sinopec, I had a tour round the oil terminal on Flotta. Neil Gordon drove me round the site and explained in detail the process of bringing oil, over 100 miles across the North Sea, in a 30-inch pipe which I could see emerging from the ground right in front of me. 'Pigs' flush water from the pipe from time to time (one was due from the Claymore field the following afternoon, pushing maybe 10,000m³ of water, at walking pace, in front of it). 'Intelligent pigs' can travel down the pipe and examine its condition. Neil did not think James Bond could break into Flotta riding in a 'pig', although he did, once, get into Eastern Europe that way.

The Flotta plant had something of a Cold War look about it. It is 40 years old after all but many of the components have been replaced, relined, repiped or simply decommissioned in that time. It reminded me of Trigger's road sweeping brush in *Only Fools and Horses*. 'Twenty years old, this brush. Mind you, it's had a few new handles and six new heads in that time,' said Trigger.

If the pig in the pipe reminded me of 007, then the control room felt a lot like a set from *The China Syndrome* (1979 – Jane Fonda, Michael Douglas and Jack Lemmon). I suppose I was in the Jane Fonda role – as a reporter visiting a nuclear plant. Happily nothing went wrong on Flotta but Jack Lemmon's character (played by Bob Heddle, the control room supervisor) did have a swivel chair on castors, a phone on the console – and was alone.

Continuing the movie theme, I have heard it said that *Local Hero* (1983 – in which an American oil tycoon attempts to buy an

Museum and oil terminal, Flotta.

entire Scottish village to build a refinery) was based on events at Flotta. In the film, the development didn't go ahead, unlike Flotta, which was built. Apparently there was one objection to the Flotta Terminal – a 16-year-old girl who thought it would destroy the island's way of life but, being not yet 18, her vote didn't count.

Orkney is a working landscape; it always has been. Electricity, telecommunications, planes, boats, roads, schools, hospitals and oil are what keep Orkney thriving in the 21st century. It is no good demonising the oil industry for the production of the fuels we all use or the plastics we all discard but we do, all of us, have to work towards a time when our planet is clean again.

## CHAPTER THIRTY-TWO

# Stronsay

'I LOVE IT, each evening, when the ferry leaves and we're safe for another night. No one can come that isn't already here, it's only us islanders that are abroad in the dark. I know it's daft, that's just how I feel. I've been here 15 years, I know all the kids and they all call me Steve. we get on great when I see them out around the island.'

STEVE WEAVER – STRONSAY SCHOOL CARETAKER

'Oh dear, I've been here so long I've nearly forgotten how to drive. I went south to visit a friend and the space outside her house needed a reverse-park. I hadn't reversed my car on Stronsay for years. There's so much space you just stop when you get where you're going and then drive off when you leave.'

PAM ROSE – TEACHER FROM SOUTH YORKSHIRE

'I've no idea where my house keys are, I haven't locked the door for years. Mind you, the lock is rusted up anyway so they'd be no use even if I found them.'

ANON

I had phoned Andrew King, head teacher at Stronsay School, and asked if I could speak to the children and staff, to get their views on island life. Like most things on Stronsay, it was no problem at all and, like head teachers everywhere, Andrew quickly delegated the task of liaising with me – to Donna Blyth. Donna had come from Scarborough so we had an instant rapport, Scarborough having been the destination of choice for my family holidays in the 1950s, before Donna was born.

Being an incomer is no impediment to enjoying life in an Orkney island. The adults I met at Stronsay School had come from Sheffield,

Shetland, Sweden and Scarborough, as well as Orkney. We discussed the balance of where people had come from and why. There may be a notion in some, southern quarters that Scottish islands can offer an escape from one's problems. In the islands, however, the belief is that it can't. They may be great places to live but if you try to escape problems, they will generally follow you. If you can leave them behind, however, then a healing is definitely there for the taking. Not everyone makes it. The general rule of thumb among locals is that they watch how you fare with the *second* winter. New arrivals are prepared for the first winter. They have heard about it. It is novel. They grit their teeth and hunker down. Chances are they will say, 'Well, that wasn't so bad, we were expecting much worse.' When the second winter sets in, however, there is the feeling of 'here we go again'. One has become sensitised; there may be dread. There is knowledge of what's to come. There's no guarantee, however, but if you make it through two winters you may be okay. (Bev and I have done two now, so fingers crossed we'll make it.)

One Stronsay folk tale is of a couple who arrived on a Thursday, unpacked the furniture van, enrolled their daughter in the school next day and looked forward to their first weekend. Saturday was 'coorse' (poor) and a conversation in the shop went something like:

'Gosh, we've arrived to some terrible weather.'

'No, this is pretty normal for May.'

They packed the van again and left on Monday.[1]

There are 35 children on roll in Stronsay School, in the care of head teacher Andrew King and his staff. I visited on a March day in 2019 – it was the warmest, sunniest, calmest day of that year so far and Stronsay was looking glorious. I had my border collie with me and she was needing a good walk by lunch time. 'Go down to Rothiesholm Beach,' they all said, so I did. There were uninterrupted white sands, blue sea and a better class of seashell

---

1 A lady I spoke to in the school said, 'Oh dear, I think it was my fault [that they left after just one weekend], it was me who made the crack about the weather.'

than I had been used to collecting on my Mainland dog walks. I wondered if, perhaps, they got picked over by fewer treasure seekers here. Whatever the reason, I went home with a bag full of perfect cockles, gapers and one or two I couldn't put a name to. Sadly, no Groatie Buckies, however, which all the children told me Stronsay was the best island for. I find everyone in Orkney has their favourite Groatie Buckie beach but is reluctant to divulge where it is. I met 30 of the school students, two others were working hard towards their exams so could not be released to meet me.

Stronsay has a population of around 350. There are two shops, one kirk, one hotel, one café, a marina, bank, ro-ro ferry pier and the village – Whitehall – a row of houses along one side of the street, which faces the bay and harbour. It is a quiet place. Inland of Whitehall, there are farms and beaches. For the purposes of this paragraph, I will call it a remote Scottish island. It is true, Stronsay is a long way from any large conurbation. Orkney's capital town – Kirkwall – is almost two hours away by ferry and, as the children were very keen to tell me, this can often be disrupted by bad weather (for 'disrupted', read 'cancelled'). There is an air service by eight-seater Islander aircraft. This is much quicker but more expensive, and seats are often taken up by teachers in term time. Stronsay belongs to the group of Scottish islands that require two sea crossings to get home from mainland Scotland. Nevertheless, if you live there, it is the centre of your world. It is Edinburgh that can seem remote.

Whether we call it remote or not, Stronsay has a set of conditions that derive from its place on the globe. All the children had an opinion which they were fluent and eloquent in expressing. Here are extracts from their written work and from recordings of them speaking to me in small groups:

## Safety

'I feel safe on Stronsay.' ARYA (6)

'Stronsay feels like a really safe place. Being able to go out with friends without parents/carers having to worry if we are safe or not.' ELLA (13)

'I also like how it feels kinda safe because we are surrounded by the sea.' TONY (12)

'When we were in Aberdeen, I was never allowed to go out shopping with my friends because it wasn't safe because there are not good people.' AIMEE (12)

'I like having the freedom of being able to go out when I want and feel safe.' AIMEE (14)

## Nature

'I feel healthy because I can run down to the beach and swim in the sea.' OLLIE (6)

'I like all the beaches because there are lots of Groatie Buckies.' MARTHA (7)

'The beaches are closer and there are lots of shells.' FILIP (8)

'I like the beaches. We get lots of shells.' CHRIS (7)

'I like the beach but I can only go in summer. I also like Lego.' NOAH (8)

'I like the beaches. They are free and there's lots of space.' LILLIAN (11)

'There are sunsets.' COLIN (7)

'The sunsets are amazing and you don't have to pay £1 for a crowded pile of sand. 95 per cent of the time you have the beaches to yourself. The northern lights are such a sight.' MELVIN (11)

'There are dark skies with stars that shine as bright as Christmas lights.' ELLA (13)

## Work – now and in the future

'I like my house because we have buffalos. We used to live in Deerness (Mainland Orkney) but the grass is better here so we brought all our buffalos across on the ferry. I don't know how many we have.' MARTHA (7)

'We lived on Eday, then Deerness and now Stronsay. I want to be an artist, a farmer or a vet. I'll be happy to go to college when the time comes.' DOROTHY [MARTHA'S SISTER] (10)

'My family and I own a buffalo farm. And over 300 chickens so people want to buy eggs – also the houses are a little cheaper which makes it a lot easier to move house.' WILBUR (9)

'When I'm older I want to be a chicken farmer or a doctor, artist or an art therapist and a police officer. I have a big list of things I would like to do and every year I cross off one or two, sometimes more.' NATHANIEL (10)

'My dad and Grandad Stronsay own our farm, I help out a lot. We have cows, sheep and chickens. It is nearly time for the lambing. When I'm older I would like to be a performer. There is lots of open space in Stronsay so I can practise a lot outside on nice days.' MILLIE (11)

'And when I grow up I would like to play for Celtic in Glasgow because that's my favourite team.' LEWIS (11)

'By staying in Stronsay and farming, it's keeping my family tradition going. Because my dad, grandad and great-grandad have all been farmers. I like spring on Stronsay because I love seeing little lambs and calves running around. Probably the two things I love about living on Stronsay are silage time and harvest time. I love going in the tractor when people are cutting silage and I love seeing combines out in the field.' AIDEN (12)

'My dad is the harbour deputy master. He works morning and night-time shifts. On a Thursday he needs to do the stay-over boat. My mum sometimes helps out my dad on the ferries but mostly she is back up if someone is ill. Also, my mum runs a vegetable garden and shop with my gran.' ERIK (14)

## Weather

'Orkney is a rainy place with some sunny days.' LIAM (9)

'On a nice day you can see Start Point Lighthouse [on Sanday] and sometimes you can see Fair Isle.' NATHANIEL (10)

'Nearly every day it is windy and raining but in the summer it is the opposite.' SAM (10)

## Friends and family

'I get to see my family.' OLLIE (6)

'I like being kind to my friends and family and to be near my granny and grandad.' STAR (7)

'I have lots of friends.' CHRIS (7)

'I have lots of friends in the school, they are the best friends in the world.' TONI-ANNE (11)

'Most of my family live in Orkney and I am very close to a lot of them. School is awesome! I have so many friends and everyone can pretty much trust everyone.' MILLIE (11)

'One of my favourite things about Stronsay is being able to go and see my family. It only takes two minutes to walk to my aunties' and it takes five minutes to get to my granny's.' AIMEE (12)

'When I was nine, my mum and dad wanted to move somewhere more quiet and safe, so they looked on a map and saw a group of islands called Orkney, then they looked it up online and they saw a house for sale on Hoy, but it was not suitable, then Mum saw a house on Stronsay so we moved on 27 January 2016.

I made lots of good friends and dad let me get a big scooter to use on the beach and off road. It is so cool that we don't have to pay to go to an overcrowded pile of sand which down south was always covered in people and toys.

I love the beaches and the amazing views. The first time I saw a seal I shouted "yay" so loud I scared it off. When I turn 12, I will go down to Chorley (near Manchester) to see my old friends and also go to McDonald's.

Sometimes the wind can close the school!' LILLIAN (11)

### Internet

'One thing which I hate probably the most is the poor internet connection.' AIDEN (12)

'One of the drawbacks is that the internet is very slow.' DAN (12)

'People here don't like the internet (speed) as it makes watching videos more difficult.' MIKEY (14)

'I don't like the broadband speed because it's slow and I have a game that is 97GB and it takes forever.' JAMIE (14)

## Gossip

'One thing I probably don't like about Stronsay is how news can spread quickly, but not accurately! But as long as you try not to tell many that should not be a problem.' MELVIN (11)

'Everyone knows everyone and gossip spreads fast.' ELIZABETH (14)

'With having a small close community gossip can spread very fast and some people can change the facts and this can make some feel uncomfortable.' MIKEY (14)

## General Likes

Our teachers (unanimous among all who expressed an opinion – which was most of them); shells; flowers; books; animals; birds; bugs; sunsets; swimming in the sea; shops (both of them); Lego; clubs; trampoline; Golden Time (free time at school).

## General Dislikes

Midges

## Conclusions

'Stronsay is a fat old mixed bag of good and bad. One minute you can marvel at the gorgeous clear night skies and the next you're swearing through your chattering teeth as you're battered with rain, wind, hail and the charming spray of salt water. We have a good school with great teachers, amazing natural scenery and an endless amount of incessant midges trying their very hardest to tear your flesh apart. Of course, they're tiny, and instead of ripping you limb from limb the little devils just ruin your limited time in the sun. Luckily enough for me, I must not be very tasty, because as long as I'm out and about with other people I just about never get bitten.

Days on Stronsay are either really good or really bad, no in between. Sometimes you're living it up! Laughing at all the people in the big cities that have to walk miles to enjoy the sand! But other times you want to tear your hair out, and when one person feels like that it's normal that everyone else does too. Especially in the case of farmers. You wait all year for something and when it finally does come you can't enjoy it because if you pause for more than two seconds you lose all the good weather and end up with wet barley or something! You can't cut that!

Internet connections is damn meh at the best of times.

But really I don't think I'd change it for the world. It's easy to bash on life in Stronsay, I certainly do. But sometimes, when you take a moment to sit back and stare out at the sea, you realise how great we have it.' FRASER (13)

'Over all I think that living here has been a good thing although I don't have anything to compare it to.' MIKEY (14)

When I told people I was moving to live in Orkney they were surprised but, once they visited us they understood. Had we moved to Stronsay it might have been a more difficult sell. Don't misunderstand me, Stronsay *is fabulous* but even the Stronsay folk would say you have to work harder at your entertainment, and make most of it yourself, or together with others in the community. The children listed beaches, swimming, helping on the farm, walking to visit friends and family, sport, performing and other activities as what they liked to do. The point being they were mostly *activities*. I didn't see any overweight children. There is television, of course, and several of them mentioned the internet but usually in the context of it being too slow for games and videos a lot of the time.

No one said there was nothing to do, as a city child might well say if he or she were to be parachuted in. They almost all wanted to stay on Stronsay or at least come back after they had been away to school and college. The Stronsay children have either been born to it or adapted to it. It is home and they love it.

## CHAPTER THIRTY-THREE

# Faray

FARAY LIES BETWEEN Eday and Westray in Orkney. The name derives from Old Norse (Faeray, meaning sheep island) and was spelled Pharay in earlier times, sometimes even North Faray to distinguish it from Fara in Scapa Flow. A look at the map shows it barely a kilometre from Eday, across Fersness Sound at its south end and just 500m from Westray, across Weatherness Sound at the north. Geologically, Faray is the higher part of a ridge running between the two larger islands. At low water, there is only about 8m in depth at Weatherness and around 15m at Ferness.

Life was not simple for Annie Harcus or Peggy Gibson who both taught at Faray School during the 1930s and 1940s. Annie was working in Westray in 1931, when she received a telegram instructing her to report to Faray School next term. Shocked but undaunted, she packed her bags and was ferried across to Faray, landing on the east side at Cleads Geo. Two men greeted her and carried the bags up to the school. Annie walked along carrying her cat in a box.

The school building on Faray was a 'but-and-ben' construction: the accommodation at one end and the school room at the other, with a communicating door in the passage. There was no running water. A tank provided water but ran dry every summer at which time supplies had to be bucketed from the croft, half a mile away. Two stone sheds with buckets provided facilities for boys and girls – teacher shared with the girls.

There were seven occupied crofts on Faray at that time: Cott, Doggerboat, Hamar, Lakequoy, Windywall, Holland and Ness. The folk on Faray had to be self-sufficient, there being no shops, church, hall, doctor, nurse or vet. Every job had to be carried out by the community, which numbered around 40. Handling the heavy jobs, such as shipping beasts across to Eday, had to be managed by almost every able-bodied man working together. Without a midwife, or even a howdie-wife, the women just helped each other deliver babies. Should a doctor be needed then one had to be collected from Eday in an open sailing boat. Weather sometimes made this impossible with inevitable consequences. Shopping for supplies, apart from what the islanders grew themselves, was also a weekly trip to Eday – weather permitting.

When Peggy Gibson arrived to teach in Faray, during the 1940s, it was her first post. She landed in Eday and hired a pony and trap to take her to a point from where the Faray boat could pick her up from the beach, there being no suitable pier. She was very lonely at first but she soon got the house sorted and got to know the children. She described them as very quiet but very friendly. Their favourite thing was to hear stories – about almost anything. They had never seen a bicycle, let alone a motor car, which were rare in the islands at that time and non-existent on Faray.

Peggy taught them well and the children responded with enthusiasm for almost every subject. Reading, writing and arithmetic were the corner stones, of course, with geography, history and drawing. There was no certificate to be had at the end of school and almost no one had any inkling of taking their education further. In Peggy's time, one lad did become a police inspector and one a deep-sea captain. Generally, they grew up to be crofter/fisher-folk and took over from their parents. The land could not feed too many mouths, however, so many had to move away. The girls may well have gone into service in the south at that time and the boys into farming or other manual jobs.

As the teacher, although only young herself, Peggy was placed on something of a pedestal by the islanders. They hung on her every word. 'The teacher says...' would be reported around the island. There was great affection for her and she never wanted for fish, lobster, partans (crabs), mutton or vegetable, plus anything else they had they shared. Without proper ovens, baking was limited to things such as girdle scones done on a hot plate.

Not long after she started in Faray Peggy was asked if she would hold a church service in the school – it being the only place big enough. It soon became a regular Sunday evening event to which everyone turned up in their best clothes. Peggy worked out some sermons, with the help of her mother who came to stay, and there was enthusiastic singing led by one islander who had a tuning fork and was appointed precentor.

With no television or radio, the islanders made their own entertainment. Peggy knew she must not have favourites among the islanders so she would visit each in turn after school each day. Most crofts had a phonograph and music was stored on cylinders, rather than the discs that would come later. She reported seven occupied crofts in her time so I'm not sure how the sharing was done. With Sunday evenings taken up with the services, that only left six nights for visiting.

Miss Gibson taught the whole island to dance. Some of the adults had spent time in Eday and elsewhere so may already have known but many, including the children learned from scratch. When the time came – Easter, harvest home and Christmas many of the Faray folk would sail over to Eday and then walk five miles to the hall for the dance. By 3.00am, they would be ready to walk and sail back again and collapse into bed as the sun was coming up – the best kind of nights out. No one lived in Faray after 1947.

On a sunny Easter Monday, I crossed from Westray pier to Faray courtesy of Jock Kent's creel boat *Crystal Sea*. We passed east of Holm of Faray to Djubi Geo, halfway down the east side of Faray. *Crystal Sea* nudged up to the rock and I stepped ashore dry-shod. There was a fixed rope up the cliff, which I ignored but, having examined the fixing point at the top, had more confidence in coming down later.

I walked up to the crown of the island, dumped my lunch bag in a safe spot and set out to explore. I have done this many times on islands all round Scotland but the thrill is always the same. Spring is the best time. The sun was warm in the clear air and the breeze not too strong. The sounds were familiar – skylarks, oystercatchers, fulmars, snipe, gulls and waves. The sun sparkled on the sea. Eday, Westray, Rusk Holm were close at hand and the hills of Rousay not far off. I had walked up from the landing

Stromness RNLI Ladies' Guild Christmas jumpers.

Harvesting the barley at Swanbister Farm for winter fodder.

View over Stromness Harbour.

January sunrise.

View of Stromness waterfront.

A favourite walk along the shore.

The author as press officer on board Stromness lifeboat during
HMS *Royal Oak* commemorations.

RNLB *Violet Dorothy and Kathleen* on exercise at
Old Man of Hoy © Barry Johnston / RNLI.

The author forgetting his age at Hoy and Walls Community School.

The author taking a breather outside the old school, Faray.

Stronsay School group – view from the playground.

Yesnaby cliffs, west Mainland.

Julie Felix after her concert in 2018.

Puffins.

The author ashore at Cava.

The Eday drum.

to the school, passed the front door and onto the road through where the school gate may once have been. The road – a fabulous grassy highway – was stone-built by the council but now covered by generations of sheep droppings. It was wide, firm, smooth and cambered. There were ditches and earthen banks on either side. No cars ever ran, this was for horse and cart, sheep, neighbours visiting and children going to school. The green track ran as far as I could see north and south from where I stood. Every deserted croft was linked. I set off north, to the ruins of Doggerboat, Cott and Quoy.

From the northernmost croft of Quoy the land slopes down to the shore and I could already see waves breaking over the shallows that would soon part to reveal a possible walk to Holm of Faray. I turned left (west) and followed the sheep paths above the cliffs and back towards the south. A succession of geos held sandy and pebbly beaches that were mercifully free from marine litter. One sandy cove was pristine, a stony bay held just one plastic bottle (bright green). I would have recovered it had access been possible for a crocky near-septuagenarian. I did manage to scramble to the shore below the graveyard, however, and recover seven bottles (which were kindly disposed of for me in the Pierowall Hotel later). All in all, I was quite heartened by the relative absence of litter on an island not normally benefiting from Bag-the-Bruckers.[1]

The cemetery is large and grandly walled like all island cemeteries. It had to be reinforced against erosion when some graves were lost to the sea. I was struck by how much room there still is in it, enough for ten times its current occupancy. The builders can never have imagined Faray being deserted and the space not being needed. Many of the stones were illegible but I read several burials from the latter part of the 19th and early 20th centuries. Between then and 1947, some may have been interred without markers.

I headed back to the landing rock and collected my gear from the school on the way. I walked through the gateway, as the

---

[1] 'Bruck' is an Orcadian word for rubbish so Bag-the-Bruckers are organised litter pickers who operate every spring to clean up beaches.

Deserted croft houses, Faray.

children had done in generations past and wondered how they had felt. I imagined them happy and laughing – I only ever meet friendly ghosts in abandoned Scottish islands.

**Further Reading:**

Annie Harcus, *Don't Tell Bab!: Early Life in Eday, Faray and Beyond – The Autobiography of Annie Harcus* (Orkney View, 1995)

CHAPTER THIRTY-FOUR

# Papa Westray – 2,000 Acres of Sky

QUIZ BUFFS KNOW Papay (Papa Westray) as the island you can reach from Westray on the world's shortest scheduled flight. It is officially two minutes, according to Guinness World Records, although I did it in just under 90 seconds. From Kirkwall to Papa Westray, it's about 25 minutes with the stop at Westray to deliver the mail. As we sat on the gravel strip, a sheep dog jumped in to see who was passing.

In April I had visited Faray, just the other side of Westray. Faray didn't make it. The community there abandoned the island to the sheep in 1947. Papay folk have no intention of going anywhere. Papay is four times the size of Faray with a community pulling together to protect and develop the island for future generations. The population is roughly stable at 85 and the development plan aims for about 100. There is a commitment to peripherality – both from the Orkney Islands Council and the Scottish Government – to invest in and sustain small island communities. The council island link officer fills a part-time post on Papay to see that council policy is applied for local benefit.

The twice-daily flight on the eight-seater aircraft brings in the mail and teachers for the school. (I sat next to the fiddle teacher coming out for the day to supplement the more regular teaching the youngsters and adults receive. It is also possible to have top up lessons via Skype.) There are six children in the school at present plus one in the nursery. Another four commute by boat to Westray and one boards at Kirkwall Grammar School during the week. Locals coming home or travelling south use the plane, as do visitors, birdwatchers, folk musicians, festival goers and just about anybody wanting to sample a special way of life.

Bev and I haven't yet been forgotten by family and friends south. Someone said, 'Everyone will visit in the first year, to see where you are, then they'll leave you alone.' We are still in that first phase so we often take friends for a day trip to Papay. Visitors number 33, 34 and 35 squeezed into the plane this time and squealed with delight at the smallness of it. I think the pilot had some difficulty in maintaining the trim as they leaned, first one way then the other, to catch the views. Number 34 timed the short leg of the flight and number 35 filmed the event for her grandson over the captain's shoulder. I forgot to mention they were all over 70.

Jonathan Ford – the Papay Ranger – met us with the minibus which had been provided by the Coastal Communities Fund – a government kitty to stimulate development in places by the sea. There are about ten road miles on Papa Westray but if you have to walk them all it can be a drain on the precious time between planes. With the bus, we were able to cherry pick stopping points for maximum benefit. Apart from that we got the Ranger's commentary which went something like:

> This is the New Pier. It's quite old now but I guess we'll call it the New Pier until we get a new one. That's the *Golden Mariana* just arriving. It carries schoolchildren to school on Westray, brings in the doctor on Wednesdays and the minister on Sundays. If it's too misty to fly back later, you can cross to Westray, get a bus down the island and the boat back to Kirkwall (Orkney's integrated transport). That's my house. That's Holland Farm – the biggest on Papay. There's the hostel, shop, community market garden that feeds the shop, school and petrol pump. This is sort of our High Street really. Here's the Old Pier, which is really old and here's the Kelp Store which is also really old but has been recently renewed to be useful again. That's a curlew, raven, wheatear, oystercatcher, eider duck. There are only four wild land mammals[1] resident on Papa Westray. Can you name them?

---

1  Field mouse, house mouse, rabbit, otter.

Jonathan came to Papay at Christmas in 2013 to see where the great auk had lived. There had been tinsel in the aircraft. He took up the ranger post two years later. He came by boat that time, thinking it the proper way to move to an island – not the first person to feel that. In his short time here, he has flitted round almost all the temporary accommodation available, making way for others to shoehorn into this tiny plot. He is currently living in Midhouse (pronounced Mothers), the former home of Papay legend, Maggie Harcus. He dreams that, one day, maybe someone will point to it and say, 'Jonathan Ford lived there, he was ranger here for 50 years and did a fantastic job for the island.'

We took advantage of the heat in the Kelp Store provided by an electric fire using surplus electricity from the turbine. The day wasn't bad but it was nice to get out of the breeze, use the loo, have a coffee and eat sandwiches.

My second-favourite building in the world (after St Magnus Cathedral) is Knap of Howar on Papay. Thought to be the oldest preserved stone house in northern Europe. Radiocarbon dating has it being occupied 5,700 to 4,800 years ago. It is older than the houses at Skara Brae which are much more familiar to people. Knap of Howar is beautiful. It stands on its own, a single farmstead with an attached 'workshop' accessed through a low passage. Archaeologists believe the workshop might have been added only a handful of years after the house was built. Someone may have said, 'You know, Betty, we could do with somewhere to store our tools and where I can do jobs.' It may have been the world's first purpose-built man-shed.

The house itself has rounded corners and is pinched in at the waist making a slightly 'hourglass' shape. There is another low doorway facing over the sea to Westray. The sea wasn't there 5,000 years ago; folk would have been able to go visiting to the neighbouring island on foot. At Knap of Howar, I always sit on the grassy bank and listen for the Neolithic conversation. I want to know what they said to each other, how they planned the day and what they worried about. I'm saving up for a TARDIS. When I get back from Knap of

Howar in 3000 BC, I'll write Part Two of this article and tell you all about it.

Jonathan took our little party to Holm of Papay on the excursion boat (Coastal Communities Fund again) to see the Stone Age burial cairn. It is a sort of long, narrow version of Maeshowe but now access is gained through a modern manhole cover and vertical ladder from the top. Inside, there are 14 burial cells and some wriggling on stomachs is required to see them all.

Holm of Papay has never been inhabited; instead, it was probably just a place of rest for the dead from the community on its larger neighbour. The Land of the Dead next to the Land of the Living.

The Coastal Communities Fund also gave money to help set up bike hire on Papay, glamping pods at the hostel and greenhouses at the market garden. There was money for the purchase of Rose Cottage from RSPB. This can now be rented out to generate income. RSPB themselves use it for a summer warden and a writer has been in residence these two winters past. Incidentally, it

Community poly tunnel, Papa Westray.

also paid for Jonathan's post to be established. I don't know how much that was but the value to an island like Papay of a Jonathan is inestimable. I'm sure I'll be back next year, with another plane-load of visitors for him to show us the puffins, guillemots, terns, bonxies, seals, the incredibly rare *Primula scotica* and to visit the Stone Age.

Meanwhile, the market garden grows apace. There are lettuces, tatties and carrots for the shop (in Beltane House, restored by Climate Challenge Fund, which also houses the six-bed hostel and eco workshop with glass crusher and cardboard briquette maker). There's a clothes rail at which you can get anything from boots to a hat for a donation or a swap. A student from Edinburgh now swaggers around town and tells the story of how he got his trilby.

There are politics, of course, on Papa Westray. The following notice appeared in the shop a few years ago:

> Suggestions for where we should put the proposed commu-
> nity shed are invited. Please be aware there may be very good
> reasons why it doesn't end up where you think it should.

After much deliberation and a public meeting, the site was chosen by the narrowest of votes. The shed was erected (to house all the shared farm machinery and the boat) and the community moved on. The glass crusher helped make the aggregate for the shed floor. With far-sightedness like that, who would bet against Papay flour-ishing into the 22nd century?

CHAPTER THIRTY-FIVE

# Hoy

MV HOY HEAD, leaves Houton around 10.00am (earlier ferries are available) and the crossing to Lyness takes 30 minutes. On fine days, I stand on deck and watch the seabirds or scan the shores of Cava and Fara for interest. During inclement weather, it is easier to sit in the car.

Moored at Lyness is a red and yellow machine, perhaps 180m long, several metres in diameter and resembling a giant sea snake. It is Pelamis – a device designed to capture wave energy and convert it to electricity. Its sister was the first to generate electricity into the national grid from deep water waves, anywhere in the world. The company behind Pelamis was formed in 1998 but wound up in 2014 after it failed to make it in the fierce competition to provide the world with a dependable wave-powered electricity generator. Pelamis has been at Lyness, going rusty, for several years. It is a sad sight but every time I see it, I give a nod to the brave entrepreneurs who risked and continue to risk everything to prove the renewable wave and tidal technology.

Some of the buildings at Lyness have been conserved and developed into a super naval museum. The museum is closed for refurbishment but, happily, the blockage to progress has been removed and visitors from 2021 will be able to enjoy the displays again. Facilities for their improved conservation, as well as a café with a view – and longer opening hours – will be provided. The old wartime recreation building nearby – a huge, barn-like structure – has been falling down for 75 years but steadfastly refuses to collapse. An artist friend commented it was grotesque enough to be an art installation in its own right. It is a listed building and so, it seems, cannot be put out of its misery.

Everything changes on reaching the Hoy Hotel at the crossroads. The island becomes a fabulous, open, wild place of few houses and many colours. About 400 people live here which is not many for Orkney's second largest island (after Mainland) at around 36,000 acres.

You now have a decision to make – left or right? It very much depends on how much time you have and your attitude to visiting places (one day might not be enough). I always go left first. On the drive down to Longhope and Brims at South Walls I sense at once I am somewhere different. There is a Hoyness about Hoy which you must feel and discover for yourself. There's the Garrison, a 1940s art deco cinema-turned-house; and the restored, gas-lit St John's Kirk.

Before crossing the Ayre to South Walls, turn right to the lovely little museum at Brims and take a few minutes to pay your respects to the eight gallant volunteers of the lifeboat TGB, killed by a huge wave in March 1969 whilst on service. Afterwards you can visit their very fitting memorial at Osmondwall cemetery in South Walls. The statue of a lifeboatman looking out to sea was cast in bronze by North Ronaldsay artist Ian Scott. Look out to sea yourself, there are the islands of Switha, Swona, South Ronaldsay and the lighthouse at Cantick Head. This is fast becoming one of my favourite views in Orkney and not a bad place to spend eternity, I always think, as I look again down at the graves.

The road to Cantick Head is potholed and not what we have become used to in Orkney. Extreme caution is needed if you drive but it's a pleasant walk. The old keepers' cottages are converted into very comfortable holiday lets, almost the last word in away-from-it-all.

Before recrossing the Ayre, there's the Napoleonic Martello tower and museum worth a look. Even if all you do is sit and enjoy your flask of tea, there is more peace. Should chocolate and crisps be running out by this point then Groat's shop in Longhope village can oblige. Indeed, should you be in need of wine, groceries, newspapers, hot drinks or a fridge then JM Groat, General Merchant is the place (the clue is in the name). The current lifeboat – RNLB *Helen Comrie*, a Tamar-class boat – is moored in the harbour. Coxswain Kevin Kirkpatrick is the grandson of Dan

Kirkpatrick BEM, who lost his life in the 1969 tragedy. Kevin's son and daughter – Jack and Stella – are also on the crew.

Lunch beckons and I recommend Emily's Tea Room, back at Lyness. Emily and her family came here a few years ago and started by building a peedie craft shop on some open ground, overlooking the sea. They soon added the tearoom and it now makes a super aiming point for any day on Hoy. Emily's is a gem. It's a delight to find it, unexpectedly, beside the otherwise empty road north.

Close by is the Naval Cemetery. This immaculate Eden is a Commonwealth War Graves site. It is always impressive to walk round and admire the beautifully kept graves from the two world conflicts Orkney has been so closely involved in. In one corner, there are two short rows of graves of sailors who died when HMS *Royal Oak* was torpedoed by U-47 in Scapa Flow in October 1939. 834 men and boys were killed but there are so few graves here because most went down with the ship, such was the shock and speed of her sinking.

Further north, the true wilderness of Hoy becomes apparent. There are views of the empty hills and glens on the left, and the islands of Cava, Fara and Rysa Little to the right (especially from the lookout seat at Lwyra). As you pass, spare a thought for the 'Woodpeckers' – Ida Woodhams and Meg Peckham – who lived a self-sufficient life, largely alone, first on Fara then Cava from 1959 to 1993.

On the brow of a hill is the tiny lochan, Water of Hoy, where you can look out for red throated divers. These attractive birds – with beautiful red and grey throat plumage in the summer – breed here regularly and it's a reliable spot to add them to your Orkney lists. Red throated divers are very prone to disturbance but this pair seem happy by the quiet roadside. There's just enough water to get up speed across the surface for take-off. Before returning to the car you must read about Betty Corrigall on the information board.

The island of Graemsay soon comes into view, with Stromness just behind. Between Hoy and Graemsay is Burra Sound where some remarkable sea trials were undertaken. It was here, in the early 21st century, that Orcadian company Orbital Marine Power (then called Scotrenewables) first put the concept of a floating tidal generator to the test. The device, the brainchild of local entrepreneur Barry Johnston, had been cooked up whilst studying at the International Centre for Island Technology in Stromness.

The success of the baby machine in Burra Sound led to a 250kW machine and eventually to the world's largest tidal turbine at 2,000kW that provided 7 per cent of Orkney's electricity through much of 2018. 7 per cent is the equivalent of Orkney getting its electricity one day a fortnight from the tides.

A left turn takes you on the even narrower road through the glen to the coastal village of Rackwick about four miles away. Many of the houses in Rackwick, an old crofting community, had fallen into disrepair but are now being restored as homes, both holiday and permanent. Composer Sir Peter Maxwell Davies lived here, before moving to Sanday towards the end of his life. It was in Rackwick that his famous meeting with Orkney's own George Mackay Brown occurred, leading to the establishment of the St Magnus Festival. From Rackwick, you may take the challenging (three hours round trip) cliff path to view the Old Man of Hoy.

An equally energetic, and I might say more rewarding, walk would be back to Moaness Pier though the glen on the other side of Ward Hill. It's a good path and takes you past Berriedale Wood. Trees hunker down in the cleft cut by the Burn of Berriedale as it runs down off the high ridge of Grut Fea. The burn joins Rackwick Burn lower down and from a distance the water course is clearly marked by the low trees that stand near it for water and shelter. The wood has been there for millennia but never spread up the hillside. One twig poked an inch above the shelter would soon be lost to the relentless wind. The habitat of Berriedale is a joy for naturalists: downy birch, rowan, aspen, willow, hazel, heather, roses, honeysuckle, ferns and blueberry all provide a rare Orkney home for some favourite woodland birds.

Just time for one last stop before the ferry: Beneth'ill Café at Moaness. Cristle and Robert came here from the Western Isles a few years ago and have established a reputation for excellence. You have to do that here. There simply is not enough passing trade to rely on a constant turnover of customers. You must be good and attract regulars to make a point of stopping in order to survive. Beneth'ill and Emily's have become destinations in their own right. Don't miss either.

Finally, if all this seems simply too much for one day then contact sisters – Roz and Rachael – at the Stromabank Hotel back in Longhope. Four rooms, restaurant with home cooking and bar, open all year. I know what I would do.

Once again, I spent some time in the island school. Here follows a small collection of the students' thoughts:

'I hate the weather, especially the wind and rain.'

'The roads have potholes. My dad has to deliver water in a tanker to Rackwick so he knows.'

'We can't recycle plastic on Hoy. A volunteer takes the school recycling to Mainland in the car. I would campaign for recycling on Hoy but I'm starting at Kirkwall Grammar School at the end of the week. Sewage is flushed straight into the sea – it makes pier jumping dodgy.'

'We would like an IKEA and fast food.'

'Also Primark.'

'The internet is too slow.'

'I don't like having to take the boat to town.'

'The playpark at Longhope is near my house and too noisy with screaming.'

'Online shopping. Some suppliers won't deliver to Hoy.'

'Our footy goals got damaged.'

With all that said there was plenty of praise for their home: 'We love the nature, beaches, cafes, places for dogs, farming, we know everyone, the Martello Tower, the Old Man of Hoy, Ward Hill, the whole outdoors, ruins and glops, freedom, bikes, peace and quiet (except at the play park – of course.)'

CHAPTER THIRTY-SIX
# Eday Unlocked

EDAY IS THE kind of place many people imagine when thinking of a Scottish island. It has away-from-it-allness in abundance. Eday is one of Orkney's North Isles and from the viewpoint at Vinquoy you can look around at the neighbours: Faray (now uninhabited), Westray, Sanday and Stronsay. Shapinsay and the hills of Rousay are not too far away. The ro-ro ferry to Kirkwall takes just 75 minutes on a straight run, but sometimes three hours when one of the boats is away for a refit. The eight-seater islander plane comes and goes every Wednesday to London Airport, the strip close to Bay of London where the island is almost cut in half by sandy bays on each side.

I had a super few days in Eday in 2019, staying in Dale Cottage close to the pier. I met Anne, the owner, briefly, but whilst I was there, she alternated between rolling fleeces at Greentoft Farm and soaking in a hot bath to ease the aches and pains of rolling fleeces. Anne's husband, Gary, also manages sheep on Calf of Eday. Everyone seemed to call it the Holm, which I guess rolls off the tongue more easily. Sheep on the Holm are Shelties and supplement their diet by eating seaweed from the shore. This is not their sole diet, as it is for the North Ronaldsay sheep most of the year, but it does give a distinct flavour popular in restaurants.

Dale Cottage is a traditional croft house on the outside but with all mod-cons on the inside. The huge flat screen TV caught my eye as soon as I walked in. So long as I can get it started, I thought, but I needn't have worried. Incredibly for these days, there was only *one* remote control and, when I pressed the button labelled '1', BBC1 sprang into life. In any case, there was the resident snowy owl to seek out so who needs the box?

Eday shop, affiliated to the Co-op, tries to have most of life's basics and essentials. It is an island shop and so depends on the

support of the islanders to be viable. Everyone has been encour-
aged to be a shareholder (most are) and the shop is run by a com-
mittee. Inside is also the post office and the coffee room – a snug
corner with sofas where one is invited to 'chill'. Going out for
coffee for the sake of it has not been an island tradition, however,
so it's a slow burn. There's a book-exchange shelf and Beth, the
supervisor, has hopes of an Eday book club being formed. The
absolute key to the success of the shop is that it is used and supported. When the van broke down recently, islanders rallied round
and provided transport for stock from the pier. As with all things
in tiny communities – where there's a will there's a way.

I had a nice chat with Ena Hewison at her bungalow, The
Noust. Ena was born overseas (in Westray) but came to Eday in
1959. Apart from brief stays in Mainland and two years in Glen-
livet, she has been in Eday most of her adult life. She appreciates
the ro-ro ferry which, she says,

> has made a big difference to life here. It means we can get
> to the town (Kirkwall) and back in a day. The old steamer
> could take several hours if it had to go by all the other
> islands. The longest trip I had was eight hours once, after
> there had been a gale for a few days and the service had
> to catch up. My mother spent all day on the boat on sev-
> eral occasions but, as she only did it about once a year she
> didn't mind. 'Once I'm on the boat, I'm on holiday,' she
> would say.

That Ena has farming in her blood is clear. She notices every crop
and every field as she travels around the island.

> There's so much grass this year that some of it isn't being
> cut. I don't like to see that, it makes the field look untidy.
> They say they don't need it though, they've enough to fill
> their silage pits and make some bales and still there's more.
> I hope they don't regret it if they run short later.

It seems scarcely credible now but Ena remembers the introduction of combine harvesters, back through binders, reapers and all
the way to scythes.

I have a picture somewhere of nine men working in a field with scythes. That whole cabinet is full of photographs which I am working through and trying to get names and dates on.

I wished I had had a few days (weeks?) to sit with Ena and help her go through her archive.

Daytime telly on wet days would not have been an option for the scythe cutters. Apart from the very limited programming back then, the generators were not normally switched on until evening. Ena said:

> We had Start-O-Matics. We switched on around teatime, but you could put them on earlier if you had washing to do. They went off at bedtime when you switched out the last light (of course this meant you would need a candle or lamp if you got up in the night). Sometimes they didn't stop but I had a piece of string from the generator shed to the kitchen window so I could stop it without going outside. Heating was from the peats but now I have an oil-fired Raeburn. Eday peat is fine though, it gives a lovely smell.

Eday peat has a reputation for quality. The blocks are dark (inkies) and give a good heat. Neighbouring islands, with little or none of the stuff, would come in boats to buy from Eday in days gone by. North Ronaldsay especially was a good customer. A contemporary of Ena is Alistair Scot who lives at Calf Sound, the exact opposite end of the island. He recalls six teams of two men each going to the peat hill and cutting enough for themselves and their neighbours in one day. There would be one man cutting and one propping up the peats to dry in the wind. As time went on though, and prosperity increased, people began to favour the easier options of coal and oil. Alistair said:

> One of my old neighbours [86] still goes to the peats but it's becoming a bit of a struggle for him so he's taken in a few coals this year. I sent away and bought an oil burner on eBay and fitted it into this Raeburn. Mains electricity [known

throughout the islands as the Hydro] came to Eday in 1980. All the cables had been laid and the houses connected, all that was required was to push in the fuses and throw a big switch somewhere. That was all done in a day and the Start-O-Matics became obsolete in an instant.

Eday Visitor and Heritage Centre has been established in the centre of the island and what a good job they have made of it. Island Ranger Laura Merry has worked very hard to curate and catalogue all the treasures that tell the story of Eday. There are comfy seats upstairs in which to sit while browsing the archives on fishing, farming and just about everything else that ever happened here. Downstairs are the main exhibits and a café at the back, open at weekends for soup, sandwiches and cakes – the inevitable island home bakes. People from far afield are increasingly drawn to heritage centres like the one on Eday to trace their roots. They come here from all corners of the globe (I know, sorry) to find out where their families originated. In this hectic world of constantly looking forward to the next computer app or political upheaval, we need to know where our roots are – to hold us up and help keep our balance.

There's a derelict kirk and I can never resist such places, to poke around, to see what treasures have been put inside for safe keeping and then forgotten about and left to the ravages of time and pigeons. Here, there is a Kawasaki motorcycle and a bass drum. 'Northern Lights Dance Band' it said on the front. I asked around and through the magic of social media discovered the band had hailed from Stronsay but had, perhaps, had a drummer from Eday which is how the drum came to be where it is. When I last heard, efforts were being made to rescue the instrument for the heritage centre in Stronsay or Eday. I hope they don't come to blows, or have a legal tussle, like the one between Leicester and York over the remains of King Richard.

Non-island folk often assume the sea to have been a barrier to communication. In stormy weather it was, and still is, but even in Orkney, there are plenty of days when Stronsay, Sanday and Westray are just half an hour away from Eday by boat. When community dancing was perhaps more popular than now folk would think nothing of a boat trip across the water to a shindig. Alistair told me of occasions when an Eday skipper would shuttle several boat loads to Stronsay for a dance, and then several loads back again in the wee small hours. Young men and women would think nothing of rowing or sailing across to visit a sweetheart.

I joined about a dozen other islanders for lunch at Roadside B&B, run by Anne Cant who had been on the island for about ten years. The Wednesday Lunch Club is an Eday institution so we squeezed into the small dining room and fell into easy conversation. People were calling me, familiarly, by my first name within a couple of minutes. The first time didn't register it was me they were speaking to. The homemade celery soup, freshly cut sandwich and apple crumble and custard with coffee to finish were delicious and the best value for £7.50 I have had in a long time.

I'm afraid I didn't speak to as many people as I would have liked, as I discovered in the first minute that the person sitting next to me was Tracy Maycock, from my hometown in East Yorkshire. We fell into that usual routine of 'Did you know so-and-so?' and 'Do you remember the old...?' etc. There are a lot of new islanders in Orkney, generally from further south in the UK. In the census of 1831, there were 961 people living here but today it is around 150, many of them 'in fae aff'.

I am often asked why I came to live in Orkney and the question is not difficult to answer: apart from peace, quiet and home bakes, I love everything about it. Others offer answers such as a slower pace of life, less traffic, clean air, water and fresh food. A sense of community they will say, not having to lock your door and room to breathe. (Old city habits die hard, however, and I locked the Eday cottage door one night on retiring. I don't think the lock had been turned since it was installed and must have rusted up. In any event I couldn't open it in the morning.)

Driving the island road during my brief stay, there was no traffic. Someone pulling in to let me pass constituted a jam and parking congestion was six cars outside the shop. There were no betting shops, factory chimneys, police stations, pubs or fast food outlets.

There were none of the things you might pass on a similar drive through any major city. No neon, no plate glass, no high-rise, no car dealerships, no graffiti or litter. Eday is a very modern place to live. It is of the present. Everyone here, natives and incomers alike, has chosen to live a life with a quality that allows rusty locks, space to breathe and lunch with neighbours every Wednesday.

Old salt works, Calf of Eday.

CHAPTER THIRTY-SEVEN

# Sanday

I AM SITTING on the ferry from Kirkwall to Sanday. So determined am I to record everything about this trip for the final chapter that I am taking the unusual step of writing on the move. I'm in the cafeteria, the Orkney Ferries speciality dish of bacon roll is to hand and the coffee is sloshing about the table. These Orkney Ferries ferries, serving the north isles of Orkney, are reaching the end of their useful lives. *Earl Thorfinn*, *Earl Sigurd* and *Varagan* are all over 30 years old and showing their age in style if not in reliability. They still do the job but the hope is they will be soon replaced by sleeker, shinier, greener boats that run on hydrogen gas generated by renewable energy technology – probably wind but possibly using wave or tidal power. MV *Alfred* has already come into service for Pentland Ferries on the St Margaret's Hope to Gill's Bay run and is thought to be the 'greenest' ferry operating in Scotland just now.

Sanday is the third largest of the Orkney islands, after Mainland and Hoy, at around 20 square miles and with an estimated population in 2020 of about 550. Etymologically it is also one of the most straightforward. Sandey or Sandøy, from the Norse, gives us 'sand island', subsequently altered to Sanday by English and Scots speakers. There is also Sandoy in the Faroe Islands. Given there is a superb collection of sandy beaches on Sanday, this derivation would seem reasonable.

My ferry is arriving at Loth, on the very southern tip of Sanday this afternoon. When the roll-on-roll-off ferries arrived, the Loth pier was adopted in preference to the old one at Kettletoft, Loth being nearer to Kirkwall and more accessible. Kettletoft had been the beating heart of the island community in former days, when almost everyone would come down to the pier at ferry times, perhaps to collect parcels, see who was coming or going and just to have a blether with whomever was about. Loth Pier does not lend itself in quite the same way. The concrete brutalism is functional but not a fuzzy, warm place to hang around.

I sailed to Sanday on Orkney Ferries' MV *Varagan* one calm Saturday afternoon. The wind had been strong the day before and would be throughout Saturday night and Sunday morning, but for now there was just a very gentle swell to the sea. When the skipper applied power to the engines and it thrummed and juddered through the ship, it took me right back to 1965 when, aged 14, I first caught the local bus from home to watch my football team in Hull 17 miles away. It was my first experience of independent travel. When the driver came out of the café at the terminus and started the engine, I got the biggest, visceral thrill. Scottish islands still do that me every time.

The boat stopped at Stronsay to drop off and pick up. We were only alongside for ten minutes. Local fishing boats were tied up for Saturday night at the pier. I always imagine fishermen relish weekends more than many other manual workers: for a few short hours they are safe.

The total journey time to Sanday was around two hours. It's a local boat, like a local train from, say, Sheffield to Newcastle. Actually, it's nothing like the train. The views of back gardens, fields of sheep and National Grid power lines do not compare with the grey sea to the horizon, low islands with croft houses silhouetted against the darkening sky.

I thought I had got to the end of the road when I arrived in Orkney but it seems there is always further one can go. I packed my suitcase and set off again, this time on the ferry to Sanday. From the terminal at Loth, on the very southern tip of Sanday, I drove up the road in the gathering dark. It was Saturday 26 October and clocks were due to go back that night. I was heading for the very north-eastern tip of Sanday at Start Point. After a couple of wrong turns, I got on the road out of Lady Village in the centre of the island, heading north. It was the first time I had navigated by road using lighthouses. North Ronaldsay was flashing away to my left and Start Point to the right. All I have to do is keep right, I thought. I found a sign saying 'Start Point Lighthouse' and turned off the already narrow road onto a narrower one. After a mile or two, the road ran out and became a sand track. The wheel ruts on either side were so deep the car was brushing the grass in the middle and I feared for any essential bits of machinery that may be sticking down below.

I reached my cottage at Park and a single light marked the door with the key in it. It was as far north as one could possibly drive a car on Sanday. The sky was black as ink and dotted with billions of stars. The streetlights of Lady Village were miles behind and I wondered if Sanday has applied for dark sky status. If not, it should, I thought. I soon got the stove lit, unpacked, switched on the electric blanket and settled down to watch *Strictly Come Dancing*. It was to be the *Halloween Spooktacular*. Bah, humbug. Still, it's nice to have a few familiar faces and a bit of jollity when one is away from a loved one, even if it was only to be for a few days.

I went to bed and, for the first time since childhood in Withernsea on the East Yorkshire coast, fell asleep counting the flashes of a lighthouse across the bedroom ceiling.

I suppose one could imagine a more remote location to live. The ferry passed Holms of Spurness as it arrived in Loth. There was a bothy on the island, now roofless and showing the iconic two gable ends of the ruined croft house against the grey sky.

There is history under every stone in Orkney. It does not unearth in the form of textbooks, CD box sets or climate-controlled glass cases of perfectly preserved and curated artefacts, however; it appears in fragments. The past is revealing itself to us through bone pieces, broken axe heads, pollen grains, rusted iron rivets and, just occasionally, through an exquisite carved whalebone plaque in a Viking boat burial, like the one found at Scar in Sanday in 1985. I suppose archaeologists wouldn't have so much

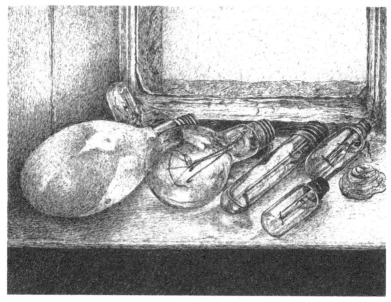

Light bulbs, Sanday.

fun if it was not like that, there would certainly be less employment for them.

The boat burial discovery at Scar began with the local farmer, John Deerness, finding a few bones sticking out of a low, eroding sea cliff near his farmhouse. He also found a small lead object, about the size of a pound coin. Both finds were reported to the Orkney archaeologist but it was not until 1991 that things started to move. In short, a Viking boat burial was suspected and an emergency excavation was organised immediately lest the site be lost to approaching winter gales. The lead object, it turned out, was not from a car battery as first thought but a Viking lead bullion weight used for weighing gold and silver on a balance scale.

The archaeologists have torn their hair out trying to make the various dating techniques applied to the grave tally to give a definite answer. There are pages of back and forth discussion about radiocarbon dating and when artefacts found in the grave might have been made. Luckily for me, I'm not an archaeologist with a professional reputation to protect so I can skip to the bottom line and say a good guess is 875–950 AD or maybe a bit later for the burial. That gives us something to programme into our imagination and ponder the circumstances of the death of the three people (man, woman and child) buried in their boat on Sanday perhaps 1,000 years to the day before I was born – on 8 May 951 (say). And why not? It's as good a date as any to work with.

I am fascinated by timelines. Trying to hold the ideas of 1,000 years (Scar), 5,000 years (Skara Brae) or 10,000 years (end of the ice age) in my head keeps me awake at night. 1,000 years is only 40 generations and 5 of those could be alive at the same time which makes it seem hardly any time at all. Some things aren't as long ago as you think. My mum remembered Wyatt Earp; Kevin Kegan could have played in the league against Sir Stanley Matthews; and finally, I was once rude about Oliver Cromwell at a party when an old lady said, 'Don't be so quick to judge. An old friend of mine said his grandfather knew The Lord Protector and he was nice.' (It works, OC died in 1658 – do the maths on the back of an envelope.)

Back to Scar and the 1,000 years since. I think it helps to plot the timeline since then in small, manageable steps, so how about:

| | |
|---|---|
| 875–950 | Scar boat burial. |
| 985 | Eric the Red sails to Greenland. |
| 1066 | William the Conqueror wins Battle of Hastings. |
| 1117 | Earl Magnus murdered. University of Oxford founded. |
| 1297 | William Wallace defeats English at Stirling Bridge. |
| 1380 | Chaucer begins his *Canterbury Tales* |
| 1485 | Richard III killed at Bosworth Field. |
| 1558 | Elizabeth I crowned. |
| 1663 | Robert Hooke uses a microscope to discover cells. |
| 1780 | Captain Cook's ships visit Orkney on way home. |
| 1833 | Slavery abolished in British Empire. |
| 1945 | D-Day. |
| 2020 | Julia's Ice Cream Shed opens in Stromness. |

In other words, the whole of modern history has happened since. Depending on how we look at it, then, 1,000 years is either a drop in the ocean or a very long time.

Enough now, back to the boat. It was 6.1m long with six planks (strakes) at each side. It was clinker built in true Viking style (over-lapping planks riveted together). Boat builders today still clinker build boats and the technique has not been improved on since Viking times. Materials and tools have improved but the design elements were fully developed 1,000 years ago. I once owned a clinker-built Orkney yole and the builder suggested I visited Oslo to see the fantastic Gokstad and Oseberg Viking ships preserved in a museum there, so I did. The construction methods were identical to my own wee boat. The Scar boat is thought to have been built, mainly of oak, in Scandinavia rather than locally.

The female skeleton, possibly of a woman of 70, had with it a sandstone spindle, a weaving batten, comb, needle tidy, fragments of a Maplewood box and a gilded bronze brooch. The star found with her was an exquisite whale bone plaque. It is 210mm wide (slightly narrow at one end) and 266mm long. Lying beside her was the skeleton of a child of around 10 years old. Its gender has not been established.

The younger male skeleton was accompanied in his grave by a sword and scabbard, a quiver of eight arrows, a bone comb and the remains of what may have been a shield. There were also 22 gaming pieces clustered so tightly together they must have been in some sort of fabric bag when buried, the bag having since rotted completely away. It is clear that one, or all three, of the individuals were of high status to have been given such a burial.

I visited Scar on a cold, breezy but sunny day in October. There was nothing remarkable to suggest a high-born Viking family had been interred there. The rollers coming in from the Atlantic would have made beaching a small, open boat very tricky.

One of my favourite tricks on islands is to visit the school. It's a good, shortcut way of finding the truth about a place (you can always rely on kids to tell you the truth). Stewart McPhail, head teacher at Sanday very kindly allowed me to spend the day talking to pupils and teachers at the school. As usual I got the low down on the weather, freedom, safety, community, internet (slowness of), McDonald's (lack of) and how much they loved living there – and going to the school.

The students had the usual mix, too, of ambitions to leave the island for college and maybe come back or maybe not. They were realistic about job opportunities and understood that there may need to be a compromise between what they wanted to do and where they could do it. Some didn't want to leave at all but stay on the family farm. Children of farmers have a very special attachment to the land and are the ones in schools, usually, with the strongest and clearest desire to stay. They are often hefted to the land and are even reluctant to go south for agricultural qualifications as a first step.

It so happened I was in school on Armistice Day so joined the whole school for their assembly at 11.00am to be reminded of that time when the guns fell silent and of the first Armistice Day just 100 years earlier in 1919. The children were impeccable in their observance. Even the two peedie, nursery children stood absolutely still and quiet, holding hands, for the full two minutes. Chloe (15) played 'The Last Post' on her cornet.

There is no substitute for being there. Whenever I have explored islands, there has always been some view, story or experience I have brought away with me to think and write about. They are usually views, stories or experiences I had never thought to have. Chloe's playing was it, on that day in Sanday. It being poppy time, I had heard the tune several times recently from all manner of professional and military musicians that had played it many more times than Chloe. I had not heard it played with more feeling.

Chloe's mum, Beverley, works in the school and she told me about Chloe whilst we waited for my bus after school:

> She is working towards grade 8 on the cornet and grade 4 on the piano so far. She started at age 7 and got grade 2 with distinction within six months. Chloe is absolutely determined to join the Royal Navy and become a musician in the Marines.

She aspires to be head bugler. Portsmouth Naval College beckons as soon as she is old enough and assuming she is accepted. The next part of the plan, after military service, is to be a music teacher back in Orkney and live on her own croft.

Beverley and husband Chaz had been paramedic and police officer, respectively, in Lancashire. For a whole variety of reasons, they brought their children to Orkney for a better life only a year ago. Beverley and Chaz are tough, they were not running away and hoping the island would solve their problems – they know it doesn't work like that. People who come to Orkney with that in mind do not stay long. Beverley and Chaz had faced and overcome plenty of challenges in their demanding jobs and saw Orkney as a new challenge which they have embraced.

Now Chloe and her sister, Katy, are responsible for four North Ronaldsay sheep: Oreo, Caramel, Lichen and Grace on their three-acre plot. The plan is to build a flock. Chloe flies into Kirkwall after school on Mondays so she can take part in music activities in

Moving kye (cattle), Sanday.

the town, including playing in a jazz band. She stays in the school halls of residence and catches up with friends who left Sanday for the big school recently. The plane brings her back to Sanday in time for school next morning. There are more lessons in the town on Saturdays.

About 500 people live on Sanday, some native, some most of their lives and some recent incomers. They all have an island story to tell but I have only made space for one. Chloe is just an example of how a super way of life can be had here by anyone prepared to work at it.

# Part Three – Living by the Sea

## CHAPTER THIRTY-EIGHT

# Scapa Beach

SCAPA BEACH IS the town beach, a short drive or walk out past the new Kirkwall hospital. It's very popular with dog-walkers but very clean. Bins are provided at the handy car park, just by the steps, and almost everyone goes armed with clean-up materials. At the bottom of spring tides, you can walk the full length, from the pier where the tugs sit all the way round to Scapa Distillery and beyond. At the top of the tide, it may be impassable but on most visits there's a curving kilometre to be enjoyed.

There are so many beaches to be visited in Orkney, each with its own charms, but Scapa is my favourite because there's always something going on. Perhaps it's the city boy still in me – not quite ready for total solitude. At one end, the tugs *Einar* and *Harald* sit waiting to see if a ship needs tugging somewhere. At the other, the Scapa Distillery is on the clifftop doing what distilleries do. On a nice day, there may be a dozen people on the beach sauntering along. One peedie chap brings his parents and the toy digger he got for Christmas. Once he tires of loading and unloading his truck with sand, he parks them on the beach and goes off for a family walk. He has no fear of them being stolen – this is Orkney, after all.

When the sea is calm, as it often is, the glassy surface buoys up flocks of wigeon, a couple of red-breasted mergansers and a few gulls. Ringed plovers, turnstones, redshanks and oystercatchers poke about the water's edge, though not usually at the same time. In winter, a dozen bar-tailed godwits visit, long-tailed ducks and, on my birthday one year, my first orca.

Beachcombing is a popular Orkney pastime. I've found a few nice shells on Scapa, though nothing rare: a Norwegian cockle and an Icelandic cyprine. There was a bag of horse feed (intact) which I gave to a passing rider, a plastic dustbin (intact, no lid) which I use in the shed. Sadly, too, there's the less appealing stuff: plastic bottles, nylon rope, a rubber glove and the odd fishing float. I have equipped myself with a shoulder bag from the charity shop and I try to pick up a few bits on each walk. There's a spring clean-up, called Bag-the-Bruck, with which a lot of folk help. A recent study identified levels of microscopic plastic particles in the sands around Scapa Flow, and Scapa beach was one of those tested. These particles (less than 5mm in size) are widespread in sands around Scotland. The levels in Scapa Flow were, surprisingly, similar to those in beaches around the Clyde and Forth. There has been some suggestion that the semi-enclosed situation of Scapa Flow, with the water not being regularly or fully exchanged by the tide, has trapped and concentrated the particles. Jenni Kakkonen – a biologist at Orkney Islands Council Marine Services who carried out the field work for the present study – now wants to examine beaches on Orkney's exposed North Sea and Atlantic coast to see if there is any truth in the rumour.

A length of nylon rope lost or discarded into the sea does not rot down like a dead fish or animal waste. It can exist in the ocean for hundreds of years. If it floats, or is cast up on a shore, and is exposed to sunlight it becomes brittle and is broken up by wave action into what scientists are calling microplastics – like the particles in Jenni's study, or even smaller. One metre of rope can produce many millions of micro-particles. The 1 metre length I picked up the other day comprised 588 individual strands of nylon, which would make over half a million 1mm particles were it allowed to break down (or even 588 million particles of 1 micrometre). So, if you collect a few short lengths of rope from the beach during your walk, you can prevent the release into the ocean of millions of potentially harmful particles.

This science is very new. In the 1950s and 1960s, the chemical DDT, used as an agricultural pesticide, was taken up by insects

which were eaten by small birds in turn consumed by top predators such as peregrine falcons. DDT did not break down as it
progressed up the food chain so ended up being concentrated in
the falcons. As a result, their breeding success plummeted leading
to their near extinction in the UK. After the banning of DDT and
related compounds, the peregrine recovered.

If microplastics pass into plankton, they can be passed up the
food chain to be concentrated in the bodies of whales, dolphins
and seabirds, then we could be faced with another DDT. We need
to be alert. I believe the plastics should not be in the sea anyway
and we should now start cleaning up our act. At the very least
there is evidence that birds such as albatrosses and fulmars are
being killed by ingesting larger pieces of plastic which they mistake for food. In any case plastics in the sea become coated with
a bio-film which harbours bacteria – often harmful if ingested by
fish, birds or mammals. The problem is serious enough to have
spawned academic interest on a global scale. Recently I attended
a lecture entitled 'Fulmars – Dustbins of the North Sea', given by
a Dutch scientist. Incidentally, attending evening lectures on local
wildlife, archaeology and history are just a few more of the many
things to do in Orkney.

This is a modern problem of our own making. Almost all the
plastics ever made are still on Earth, somewhere. In the 1950s we
made about a million tonnes every year; now that figure is over
100 million.

CHAPTER THIRTY-NINE

# Diving in Scapa Flow

ORKNEY WAS THE base for the British Home Fleet in both World Wars. It was also the place of internment of the German Fleet in 1919. A significant number of these mighty ships still lie on the floor of Scapa Flow and elsewhere around the Orkney coast. They arrived there by a variety of causes: enemy action, accident and even at the hand of their own crews in the case of the German ships. Orkney is now the dive capital of the world for people wanting to come and explore these wrecks. Stromness is a base for dive boat owners, shops, restaurants and instructors who cater for visiting divers. Diving then is a significant part of our way of life.

Walking on Scapa Beach, my attention is usually held by birds, boats and other dog-walkers on the land, or at least on the surface of the sea. What lies beneath is a whole other story.

You may be forgiven for thinking the painfully slow haggling and falling out over Brexit is a new phenomenon in European politics. You'd be wrong. We celebrate Armistice Day every year on 11 November and I suspect many of my generation (myself included) have never really stopped to consider the exact meaning of that word. We just thought it meant peace – the end of WWI. The war is defined as 1914 to 1918 and the first Armistice Day was in 1918, so it seems a fair assumption.

In fact, WWI was not formally concluded until the Treaty of Versailles was signed on 28 June 1919 and came into effect on 10 January 1920. The period from November 1918 until June 1919 witnessed one of the most bizarre episodes in military history ever – and it took place just outside the room wherein I sit writing this.

It was agreed as a condition of the armistice that the German Fleet would allow itself to be interned in a neutral port until the fine details of the peace could be agreed. Somehow the ships – 72 of them – ended up in Scapa Flow, Orkney, hardly a neutral port since it was the wartime base for the Royal Navy. Nevertheless, they were brought under Royal Navy escort and corralled here.

They were huddled together, some roped in pairs and anchored around the tiny island of Cava at the north western end of the Flow. It may have been an oversight when the anchorages were allocated but the German flagship, the battleship SMS *Friedrich der Grosse*, was positioned due north of Cava and so not in direct line of sight with the British supervising ships to the south. Flag signals therefore had to be relayed by the battlecruiser SMS *Seydlitz* anchored south west of Cava.

Life on board the interned ships was grim. German naval vessels of the time were not designed to be lived in as Royal Navy ships had always been. They were intended to sit in port, with the crew in barracks ashore, only venturing out for short sorties close to Germany, so facilities were very limited. Furthermore, the men were never allowed ashore or even to visit neighbouring ships. Morale was already low when they arrived and became even worse. These men were not prisoners of war however, Germany had not surrendered at this point – both sides were simply observing a truce and so Admiral von Reuter, the German Commander in Chief, took every opportunity to send men home to Germany and reduce the burden on the ships in Scapa Flow. At British insistence the interned ships were supplied from Germany by a regular shuttle of supply boats and they would take men away with them.

Von Reuter's big concern was that the peace process would fail and hostilities resume. That being the case, his ships would immediately be seized by the allies with the potential to be used against Germany. More than 70 of the most modern warships in the world suddenly switching sides was unthinkable to him. Even the more likely outcome – a German surrender – would leave the ships to be disposed of by the allies. Germany was in a very weak position with almost nothing to bargain with. France and Italy wanted a share of the fleet, to show their people they had made tangible gains from the conflict. America would have been happy with that so that British sea power wasn't added to. Better to send the whole lot to the seabed, he thought, rather than any of the alternatives. After all, he reasoned, any naval commander at any time in history would rather see his ship scuttled than fall into enemy hands.

So it was that Admiral von Reuter made secret plans with a few of his trusted officers to scuttle the entire fleet if the time came. It did come, on 21 June 1919. Fearing the worst from the negotiations taking place in France Reuter ordered engineers to move through the ships and open all internal doors and hatches. It has been suggested, although never proved, that some were welded open to prevent the British authorities saving the ships. All that remained was for the sea cocks to be opened to start the flooding and inevitable sinking.

By coincidence, the British flotilla was at sea that day on torpedo exercise. Also, quite by chance, the day was chosen to escort 400 Orkney school children on a boat trip to 'review the fleet'. They were loaded on board the Royal Navy ship *Flying Kestrel*, from the quayside in Stromness, and sailed off for a day trip they would remember for the rest of their lives.

The sea was calm and the weather glorious. *Flying Kestrel* passed close to many of the huge German ships. There was waving between the children and the sailors (not all of it friendly) and they passed on, further south, all the way to Lyness where they turned round.

Von Reuter gave the order. The flag signal 'Paragraph 11, confirm' was hoisted and copied from ship to ship (which took a while, of course, because of line of sight difficulties). The ships began to fill with water, settle and sink. Some went quietly and serenely and remained upright, some went down by the bow or stern and some rolled over. There was loud gushing and hissing of air out through upper hatches as the water rose inside. Oil flooded out, anything that was not tied down and would float did so. Whirlpools and eddies formed as ships disappeared. The sea around *Flying Kestrel* was chaos. The children were wide-eyed, some thinking an entertainment had been laid on for them. The crew, however, were concerned not to be caught up in the turbulence. On top of all that the naval commanders suddenly wanted *Flying Kestrel* back to help try to prevent as many ship losses as possible. She rushed into to Stromness, disembarked the children and joined the fray.

No one drowned. The sailors took to the boats and made it to safety one way or another. There was small arms fire, and even some shelling from the British ships in the confusion. Nine German sailors were shot, in various attempts to prevent the scuttle. It is clear that some people did not cover themselves in glory that day. Some justified the shooting by saying a state of war now existed again, although how an enemy destroying his own weapons could be deemed aggression was not made clear. One German boat load of sailors made it the short distance to the island of Cava and was turned away by women with pitchforks. Cava is uninhabited now and such a thing is hard to imagine as I look out of the window.

By tea time it was all over and 54 of the ships lay at the bottom of Scapa Flow. Some out of sight and some with their upper works still showing. A few had been beached by the British who had got to them in time. If nothing else the Grand Scuttle, as it became known, preserved German honour and saved the allies having to make a decision. The British authorities were privately relieved, although they protested very loudly at the time.

Admiral von Reuter eventually made it home to Germany, via a prisoner of war camp in England and then out through the port of Hull. He received a hero's welcome and was promoted. He died in 1943 and so was spared seeing Germany defeated a second time.

The story of the German fleet did not end there. During the inter-war years a huge salvage operation was mounted and many of ships were re-floated and towed away to be scrapped for their (very valuable) metal content. Remember they were not badly damaged. All that was required for many was to close up the sea cocks and pump out the water – the hulls bobbed to the surface, upside down, ready for towing. Aileen Gray, now living in Stromness, was living as a child on the island of Stroma before WWII, where her father was lighthouse keeper. She remembers being called out of bed one summer evening to go outside and watch the spectacle of the huge, upside down hulks, like giant whales, being towed away. It is even suggested that Adolf Hitler bought some of the iron during the 1930s as he commenced his rearmament.

In a fascinating footnote to the story of the sunken ships it is a fact that a few of them were salvaged *after* 1945. When the bombs fell on Hiroshima and Nagasaki they were protected from the global fallout by several metres of water and so were not contaminated. That metal is now much sought after by the makers of sensitive scientific equipment. Some has even been used in space.

Fast forward to 2020 and the sunken vessels are still sought after – as recreational diving destinations. There are three battleships and four cruisers lying at easily accessible depths, and all within one hour steaming from Stromness where the dive charter boats are based. The *Jean Elaine, Sharon Rose, Halton, Karin, Invincible, Huskyan Valkyrie* and *Valhalla* are available throughout the summer months taking groups of up to 12 divers out to the wrecks. Sometimes a dive club will take over a whole boat for the week. At other times the skipper will make up a load from smaller groups of friends. To extend the season the boats may well go off to Shetland, Norway or the Scottish west coast.

Scapa Flow is seen as the ultimate destination for UK diving. There is nowhere quite like it – probably anywhere in the world. It is a rite of passage for divers. They learn the basics in swimming pools and quarries then, when the club elders think they are ready, will be included on a trip to Scapa. They may live for a week on the boat itself (nowadays many seek greater comfort in waterfront apartments or B&Bs. Boats have also moved up-market with their catering.

Divers might come for the group bonding, evenings in the pub and, of course, the world-class diving. Some just come for the peace and quiet – and the diving. Groups staying on the boat might arrange a night in The Sands Hotel bar on Burray or maybe a night anchored close to the pub in Longhope – or both.

Divers staying in Stromness may enjoy a hearty breakfast in Julia's Bistro on the harbour, before being delivered to a marker buoy over one of the wrecks. All they then have to do, once in the water, is follow the shot line down to the ship and begin exploring. Visibility can vary, depending on plankton levels, algal blooms and currents, from 2m (nothing much to see without shining a powerful torch onto a few details) to 15m (fabulous). The average is 6–8m, which gives ample opportunity to see much of what they came to see. In a typical Scapa week, the visiting divers can expect to enjoy two dives a day and see all the main wrecks.

The ships have been down on the seabed for 100 years. They are rusting away and covered with anemones, dead men's fingers and barnacles. They are artificial reefs in effect and quite a bit of the shape has to be imagined from the biotic covering layer. If the ship settled upside down then the guns and upper works are often distorted and out of place. This all adds to the need for imagination and good homework to interpret what the diver is seeing. Some wrecks are off-limits to recreational divers. HMS *Royal Oak*, HMS *Vanguard* and HMS *Hampshire* are all war graves. *Hampshire* hit a mine in 1916 and went down with the loss of 737, *Royal Oak* was sunk in 1939 by a torpedo from a U-boat with 734 killed and *Vanguard* blew up at anchor in 1917. All but two of the 845 on board were killed.

In 2019, a volunteer dive team was granted permission to thoroughly survey the wreck of HMS *Royal Oak* in advance of the 80-year anniversary of her loss. The last survivor of the sinking – Arthur Smith – died in 2016 but the HMS *Royal Oak* Association keeps in touch with the families and a commemorative wreath laying is held every year over the wreck. Royal Navy divers also place a white ensign on the wreck at the same time.

Andy Cuthbertson, owner and skipper of the *Jean Elaine* dive charter boat regularly travels out to the wreck sites. Andy very kindly let me ride along one fabulous day in May, to see what the divers get up to. We motored out of Stromness harbour in the *Jean Elaine* and took up position, just east of Cava, where the day's diving was to be. I was in sight of my house the whole time and could even see our washing on the line. The dive support boats do not anchor over the wrecks. The divers are delivered to a buoy on the surface indicating the shot line which is secured to the wreck below. Divers simply jump in and follow the line down. It helps they know exactly where on the wreck the line is fixed (Andy and others secure them at the start of each season). Once they swim away from the line they have to think about where they are a lot more.

Andy has been in the diving business for 31 years. He hails from Northumberland where he was a lumberjack originally. He has dived all over the world. At other times of the season he takes his boat further afield to Orkney's northern isles and also to Shetland. The season was just starting in May and the skippers were expecting a lot of activity in June for the centenary of the scuttle on the 21st. As we chugged out to the wrecks Andy was on the radio to all the other boats liaising over who wanted to dive on which wrecks. They try to keep to no more than two boats per wreck and will rotate round the different sites as the day progresses.

Tim (62) was looking forward to his 21st and 22nd dives respectively. His instructors (two) were taking very good care of him, making sure he understood all the safety rules. His equipment was checked and the outline of the dive gone through so he would know what he was seeing when he got down there. On this day, visibility was about average and okay to see some fine detail on the ships, even so it helped Tim to know in advance what he was looking at. There is no voice communication under water, of course, so everything has to be done with hand signals. The lesson went something like this:

> The shot line is tied to the bridge. From there we'll head
> to the bow control tower, shine our torches in and look

through the door. There are two guns, then two anchor capstans, on one of which we will see the shaft and manual turning wheel. We can read some of the writing on the gun instructions for opening to load the shell. We'll come under the lifeboat davits, past the back end of some guns. There may be some current in which case we'll adapt the dive. There's also an estate agent's sign and a modern toilet, recently installed by some wag diver.

Andy commented that everything was a lot more politically correct these days and there was little room for liberties of that nature.

Enormous care was taken of Tim. 'I'm waited on hand and foot,' he said. 'Some dive masters follow the sun, going out to Thailand or somewhere at the end of the UK season. Some just go home, get some work and see the family until the sun returns.'

Scapa has a bit of a reputation for being a dive for Hard Men. Deep, Dark and Dangerous. 'Nothing could be further from the truth,' said Andy over lunch in the saloon of *Jean Elaine*:

> There are deep dives if you want them but we had a group of novices and their instructors last year. They came for the week and dived on wrecks twice a day. There are drifters, aircraft, escort vessels, steam trawlers, passenger ferries and minesweepers. Many are in less than 20m of water and some in less than 10m. They cut their teeth on these shallow dives and earned a go at one of the big ships, a bit deeper, at the end of the week. They were elated and went home very happy. Many people come back time and time again. They want to do all the dives possible and then start again at the beginning.

There are so many stories here. SMS *Bayern*, a 28,080-ton battleship, went down by the stern when she was scuttled in 1919. There she lay, upside down, until salvage operations commenced in 1933. Unfortunately, a bit too much compressed air was pumped in and she shot to the surface rather too quickly. To further complicate matters the four main armament gun turrets had not been secured to the hull for the lift (at a combined weight of 2,500 tons they were not normally fixed to the deck, they just sat on bearings) the ship floated upwards and left them on the seabed. Lighter, now, and with her centre of gravity altered she bobbed up like a cork. The further she went, the lower the pressure and so the more the air inside expanded – adding to the buoyancy. *Bayern* broke the surface like a breaching whale, almost under a salvage vessel. Sadly, she rolled a bit, filled with water and sank again. The story reminds me of those cartoons where someone tries to hoist a barrel with a pulley – you know the ones I mean.

SMS *Bayern* was eventually salvaged and towed away for scrapping. The four gun turrets, however, were never recovered and can still be seen, lying upside down in their original pattern and set in a depressed outline of the ship. There's a similar but shallower depression a few metres away where *Bayern* sank to the second time. Shallower because it wasn't there so long and had less time to compact the seabed.

On a day out with Andy everyone gets two dives of about an hour each depending on the depth of the wreck, experience and any tidal current that may be flowing. He does not advise doing all three because of the water temperature and the 'stress' of wreck diving. By stress I guess he means excitement, but also the pressure of avoiding jagged metal, dark holes, anchor chains etc. Immediately on coming back aboard – via the powered lift – each diver is handed a mug of hot tea or coffee. They dry off and rest before the next dive. There may even be a light lunch.

Some divers chose on the basis of what they had done before. Tim, a novice, had the choices made for him by his instructors. They had to consider the depth and the ease, and safety of diving on the chosen wrecks. The three dives on offer that day were: SMS *Kronprinz Wilhelm*; SMS *Cöln II* and SMS *Karlsruhe II*. The acronym: SMS (Seiner Majestät Schiff) is roughly equivalent to HMS in the Royal Navy.

SMS *Kronprinz* was launched in 1913 and had *Wilhelm* added to her name later, to mark the 59th birthday of Kaiser Wilhelm II. She was a battleship dreadnought. On 21 June 1919, along with most of the rest of the German fleet she was scuttled in Scapa Flow by her own crew. She sank at 1.15pm, settling upside down on the sandy seabed. She had been anchored a few hundred metres from SMS *Markgraf* and SMS *König* (her two sister ships). All three went down and all still lie close by one another.

After changing hands several times, between various salvage companies they all received protection as Maritime Scheduled Ancient Monuments. Although diving is allowed on the wrecks they must not be interfered with in any way nor have items removed. *Kronprinz Wilhelm* lies in 38m of water. She looks like a dead whale torn at by scavengers for the tastiest morsels. What 100 years of salt water immersion would fail to achieve a few sticks of explosive accomplished in a few seconds. Along with many of the other wrecks in Scapa Flow (others having been re-floated and towed away for salvage) there are holes where the more valuable non-ferrous metals were blasted out: torpedo tubes, condensers, turbines etc. Just as a bear takes a bite out of a salmon and throws the rest away.

SMS *Cöln II* was a light cruiser launched in 1916. There was some debate over the spelling of the name: *Cöln* or *Köln*, but a quick look at the recovered bell in Stromness Museum settles it. The most intact of the four Kleiner Kreuzers (light cruisers) she rests in 36m of water on her starboard side. She has a bite taken out of her stern where salvors got at the turbine and boilers. Apart from that she looks ready to get up steam and sail away at any moment.

*Cöln II* is one of the most rewarding dives in the flow. At an ideal depth for divers of all abilities they can spend a relatively long time exploring the wreck with minimal decompression times as they surface.

SMS *Karlsruhe II*, launched in 1916, is another of the light cruisers. She lies in roughly 25m of water, off the lighthouse on the northerly tip of Cava. I can see the exact spot two miles away, across the fields and Scapa Flow. It is an enormous privilege to live and work in such a beautiful and historic setting.

There is often a frisson of adventure in the various writings about the Scapa wrecks: 'Two features that should not be missed are the 5.9-inch guns and the deck capstans forward,' says Rob

Macdonald in his excellent *Dive Scapa Flow* (the centenary edition of which was published by Whittles Publishing in 2017). As a lad raised in the 1950s and 1960s, I understand this absolutely.

*Karlsruhe* was ravaged by salvors having been built in 1915 when brass and other valuable metals were still readily available. The bridge, made wholly of brass plate, was a valuable target for the metal men.

In 2010, divers on the Karlsruhe recovered some steel boxes and brought them to the surface. They were found to contain a huge stock of postcards the navy had provided the sailors for the purpose of writing home. None of the cards was written but the small selection of images (a ship in one and a couple of children in another) was just a tiny snapshot of life on board 100 years ago. The cards are in Orkney Archive, conserved for posterity and where I viewed them whilst writing this.

Strictly speaking the cards should not have been removed from the wreck under its protected status but it makes no kind of sense to me to have left them (they are already in a very fragile state and would certainly not have survived another 100 years) when they can be in the museum. Over the years of recreational diving there have been many objects removed into 'private collections' – brass port holes seem to have been a favourite. Even now there are objects lying around, especially on the deeper wrecks that could be removed. It has been suggested that an organised gathering and removal into a proper, conserved collection somewhere – an Orkney museum being the obvious choice – might be appropriate.

If you are an experienced diver, and happy to go out without an instructor, you could go with Andy himself. The *Jean Elaine* was built in Fraserburgh in 1956 – larch on oak. Originally named *Present Help* she was rechristened *Jean Elaine* after the second owner's daughter. Andy is the third owner. *Jean Elaine* is a 72ft drifter and followed the herring from Shetland to Lowestoft every season. She came to Orkney in 1994 and is now classed as a charter boat. She has worked from St Kilda, round the west and east coasts of Scotland and the northern isles.

Recovering a diver, Scapa Flow.

CHAPTER FORTY

# Birds and a Few Mammals

ORKNEY IS A bird watcher's paradise. In this chapter on birds (and a few mammals) I examine this claim and ask some questions about that state of our bird populations in 2020, how they came to be where they are and where they are headed. Wildlife tourism is hugely important here.

People come to Orkney from all over the world to watch birds. They rave about the islands as a bird-watchers' paradise. Hen harriers, short-eared owls, red-throated divers, white-tailed eagles, curlews, redshanks, arctic skuas, bonxies (great skuas) and on and on. They are all fabulous birds. Birdwatchers from Kent or Wolverhampton or Chipping Sodbury may not have seen any of them before. They will be, in twitchers' parlance, life ticks – birds they are seeing for the first time. They will go home delighted. Their Orkney list will be superb. One of each will do. One hen harrier, one owl, one diver and maybe even a corncrake calling, late at night. (Birdwatchers will accept simply hearing a bird as a tick if the ID is definite. Those among you who have never seen a cuckoo can now add it to your life lists because I'm sure you will have heard one.) They will tell their friends what a great place for birding Orkney is, and it is.

Being a great place to tick off a few rarities, however, is not the same as being a great place for birds. You go home and report a hen harrier, but how many hen harriers *should* you have seen? You saw the teeming cliffs at Marwick Head but how many kittiwakes were there? 100? 1,000? 10,000? How many *should* there have been? How many were there before global warming, over-exploitation of sand eels and ocean acidification came along. On Fair Isle, between Orkney and Shetland, they count kittiwakes every year. There used to be 10,000 and they took two weeks to count on all the cliffs. Now there are 500 and they count them before Monday lunch.

Corncrakes used to be commonplace. There are recipes for corncrake pie. Now we plant nettles to protect them and folk are delighted if they hear one. We congratulate ourselves at adjusting farming practices in small pockets of land to encourage corncrakes (cutting silage later in the season and leaving nettles for cover are chief among them). One crofter I met some years ago said, 'Get a corncrake on your croft and you can retire on the subsidy.' All these measures are good and welcome but we must not forget we have a long way to go.

Some people argue that encouraging corncrakes in the UK is a waste of time and money. Corncrakes are plentiful elsewhere in Europe, they are not endangered, they say. True, but the counter argument is that, by expanding their range into the UK, we are providing a buffer against some environmental crash in Europe.

Jenny Diski, in her book *What I don't know about animals*, draws our attention to the northern white rhino (there are two left – both female. Sudan, the last male died aged 45 in 2018. He had been under armed guard for years to protect him from poachers). She says few of us will ever see one. We all think it would be A Bad Thing were they to become extinct – which they probably will. How much would we actually care, in the end? We cling to the idea of northern white rhinos roaming in their natural habitat but what are we prepared to do to prevent their extinction and how many tears will we really shed over them when it happens?

For the northern white rhino read the great auk, the dodo, the passenger pigeon and on, back into the mists of time. One of the more selfish arguments for conserving species diversity is that useful substances, as yet undetected, may be found. A classic discovery, as long ago as 2,400 years, was that chewing leaves of the willow tree could alleviate pain. The Bayer Company called this 'aspirin' in 1899 and now about 120 billion tablets are consumed, worldwide, each year. Imagine if Iron Age or Bronze Age farmers had eradicated willow trees before this discovery had been made. What if the once-and-for-all cancer cure was in the Saint Helena

Olive Tree – the last specimen of which died in 2003? What if a precursor of a cure can be found in the urine of the northern white rhino?

The great auk was flightless. It was a relative of the present-day auks – puffins, guillemots and such. It looked like a large version of the razorbill. Being flightless, it filled a niche in the northern hemisphere similar to that filled by penguins in the south.

There is some dispute over when the last great auk was killed. Being large, meaty and flightless, it was easy prey to generations of seafarers who collected them in thousands to restock their ships' larders. In the tiny Orkney island of Papa Westray, the last two great auks – known as the king and queen of the auks – were killed in 1813, shot by William Foulis on Fowl Craig. One of the last Orkney birds is currently stuffed and resides in the Natural History Museum. Jonathon Ford – the Papa Westray Ranger – is working on the creation of a bronze statue of the bird to bring back to Fowl Craig.

There is a widespread acceptance that, so long as there are birds to be seen, and a few examples of each species, then that is enough. Wild birds, it seems, are not like food or water, sunshine, hospital beds or school places. There isn't a number we aspire to have. We are not constantly craving more – like wages, pensions, electronic devices or TV channels. As long as they are there in sufficient number and variety for the twitchers and casual holiday birdwatchers and walkers with binoculars then that seems to be okay.

I once fell into conversation with a chap at a party whom I had never met. It being Orkney it was no surprise when renewable energy cropped up.

'The barrage across the Severn Estuary or Cardiff Bay will be a good thing, if they ever build it,' he said.

'Does it bother you that half the wild birds will be lost?' I asked.

'It'll be okay, there'll still be the other site for them' was his answer.

Whilst it may be possible for some birds to move to the other site, generally they will not, for the very simple reason it may be full. Food supplies and nest sites are limited and if there's no opportunity to muscle in then homeless birds will disperse further afield in search of a new home which they probably won't find. Of course, with the decline in the number of nest sites the species population will decline over time. Seabirds and waders are quite long lived. Thirty years is not uncommon and I heard of a fulmar recently that was still going strong in 2006 after having been ringed as a chick in 1951 (the year I was born). If it's still out there it will be 68. Just imagine, a bird, swooping and gliding over the world's oceans, in all weathers, with only a break each summer to sit on a cliff ledge, whilst I did everything I have ever done. I was born, grew, played, went to school, had a family, a career, retired and wrote this book – all the while that fulmar searched over the waves for food. I wonder if it has any sense of the changes during its life. Is it aware of changes in ocean temperature, acidity, plastic pollution, fish stocks or shipping? Does it know that its kind have successfully colonised the whole UK coast, but is now in decline? If adult birds are failing to breed, it can be quite a long time before the full effect is noticed at a colony.

We know that humans, first hunter/gatherers then farmers, arrived in Orkney some time after the last ice melted around 11,000 years ago, but when did the birds arrive? Which birds and how many were there?

Birds are better equipped for crossing water than people, and their requirements for food, shelter and comfort are somewhat less, so it seems likely they arrived, at least to explore, soon after the ice left. As soon as a covering of plant and insect life was established, with associated nuts and berries, then the birds could come. Seabirds could live here even earlier, all they need is a rocky ledge, grassy burrow or scrape of shingle. All the food they need is in the sea.

So, what did the bird-scape look like around Orkney farms, hills and coast 5,000 years ago? There is very little archaeological record. Famously we know there were white-tailed eagles.

Remains of 8–20 such birds were found at Tomb of the Eagles, at the southern tip of South Ronaldsay. They were placed in the tomb when it was approximately 1,000 years old (about 4,000 years ago). The last white-tailed eagles to breed in Orkney were 150 years ago – until now. In 2018, a pair arrived in Hoy and successfully fledged two chicks, on the cliffs overlooking the road through the valley to Rackwick. Even better news is that the adults arrived under their own steam, they were not artificially re-introduced as some have been. It shows the habitat of north Hoy is attractive to them.

Today's eagles have been seen taking fulmars and mountain hares to eat. One bird sat on the ledge and nonchalantly reached out a taloned leg to pluck a fulmar from the air as it flew past. In modern times fulmars only spread round the UK coast, from St Kilda, beginning in around 1850. If there were no fulmars in Orkney in Neolithic times then the eagles would have had to eat something else. It seems likely there would be no shortage of prey species among the seabirds. Eagles are top predators, of course, so their presence indicates a healthy food pyramid of hares, birds, small mammals with a supporting cast of plants insects and fish. Plenty of sand eels and plankton, cool water, non-acidic and plastic free.

In the next valley over from the modern eagle nest is Berriedale Wood. Berriedale is a delight. It nestles in the bottom of a deep ravine with a stream running through to keep its roots nicely watered. There are downy birch, rowan, aspen, willow and hazel in the canopy, with heather, roses, honeysuckle, ferns and blueberry below. It is a broad-leafed woodland, isolated from other such places but big enough to support small breeding populations of woodland birds.

There are very few woodland birds in Orkney, for obvious reasons, but they might have been here once. The ubiquitous wren, robin, blackbird and song thrush are here and a glance through the British Trust for Ornithology Breeding Atlas shows blue tit, coal tit, long-tailed tit, tree creeper, dipper and mistle thrush all breeding throughout Britain including up to the north coast of the Scottish mainland, but not Orkney. Could they have been common here when we had more tree cover 5,000 years ago? Two birds much associated with farmland – yellowhammer and corn bunting – both formerly bred in Orkney (they are shown in the 1976 breeding atlas) but only odd sightings in recent years according to Orkney Bird Reports.

We know there has been persecution of birds in Orkney, as elsewhere, for 'sport' and hunting for food. There has been habitat loss, mainly through the draining of land for agriculture, removal of heather during peat-cutting and removal of trees, again for farming and to supply firewood. Orkney will also have suffered, like everywhere else, from the use of pesticidal chemicals from the 1940s onwards.

The attitude to wildlife has changed massively in recorded history. One only has to read accounts of bird life written 100 years ago to get the picture.

A local friend lent me a copy of *A Fauna of the Orkney Islands* by TE Buckley and JA Harvey-Brown (1891). It makes interesting reading:

> The great auk is extinct. The ptarmigan has gone from Orkney. The sea eagle is an occasional visitor, the golden eagle even rarer. All directly extirpated by man. Others have gone indirectly by cultivation drainage. Attempted introductions of pheasant, partridge, red-legged partridge and black game have probably all failed. [In 2016, pheasant was reported as a common breeding bird with small numbers of red-legged partridge and red grouse.]

Incidentally, there were 29 inhabited islands in Orkney in 1891, compared with about 20 today. It hasn't only been the birds that have seen their range shrink. Here are a few more quotations from Buckley and Harvey-Brown:

> In former times nearly all the islands were covered with heather, which is now fast disappearing. The natives strip the ground with sharp spades for fuel [peat] or roofing [turf]. The roots being thus destroyed – an unsightly practice – we wonder the proprietors allow.

In 1832, when kelp production ceased to pay agriculture was promoted through 'Improvements' which included the clearance of people from the land, drainage and the introduction of sheep.

Grouse, golden plover and short-eared owl are getting crowded out.

The short-eared owl is a poster bird for Orkney visitors and residents alike but its numbers fluctuate even today. It is described by the bird report as an uncommon breeding resident. The arrival of stoats from the mainland – probably introduced accidentally, perhaps in loads of feedstuffs etc – has coincided with a fall in short-eared owl numbers. Stoats predate another Orkney treasure – the Orkney vole – which is a staple of the owl and hen harrier and hence may impact owl breeding success. The short-eared owl was described as 'plentiful in Hoy' but then:

we got a nest of six eggs in 1883 – the only one we could find. The pair probably bred again as neither was killed.

The eggs were probably taken for sale to collectors. The authors felt it necessary to comment neither bird was killed since one could have reasonably expected one or both to have been shot – for sale to taxidermists and collectors again:

A Mr Dunn, the naturalist in Stromness paid 6d [six old pence – 2½ new pence] each for eggs of hen harrier or short-eared owl. They declined in consequence. The burning of heather for pasture also resulted in owl decline.

Draining of moors drives out the snipe, once extremely numerous.

Shepherds' dogs and cats reduce lapwing, ring dotterels etc which once swarmed.

But when the area is so comparatively small and the population increases, agriculture must push ahead to the detriment of the feroe nature [sic].

Mr Watt of Skaill reported to Buckley and Harvey-Brown:

> The Loch of Skaill and Bay of Skaill have declined for birds in the last 25 years, especially the small waders and also phalarope, greenshank, ruffs etc [all three described today as rare or passage migrants – poignantly noting they have bred].

> Turnstones were pretty numerous between 1863 and 1870 but haven't been seen for years. Sandlarks and dunlin are small in numbers compared to flocks that used to frequent our shores. They have fallen off owing to cultivation of their former, quiet breeding grounds. Snipe, redshanks, green plover [lapwing] were plentiful but now few, owing to swamps being drained and turned into fertile fields.

Perhaps the most shocking and incomprehensible reports were of the type:

> I shot a couple of brace of knot in 1868 out of a flock of ten.

> I shot a greenshank and a reeve [female knot] last year [1883].

> 100 dozen eggs taken from Sule Skerry/Stack in 1890 and sold in Stromness.

I suspect these were seabird eggs taken and sold for food. The annual harvest of seabird eggs was widespread through Scotland's islands – famously St Kilda – and was more or less sustainable at the time:

> In 1883 the gamekeeper on Rousay shot the male hen harrier from the only nest he found.

> In 1882 Mr Spence obtained eight hen harrier eggs.

> Their principal food is the common vole [in fact the Orkney vole, which is a different species and endemic to Orkney]. And on account of the numbers of this animal they kill I think they should be preserved [he meant protected – perhaps out of the mistaken belief that voles are pests].

> People gladly killed young birds and took eggs to protect chickens.

Buckley and Harvey-Brown had quite a lot to say about eagles:

> We were informed by a man who has taken their nests for several years past that they both lay 2–3 eggs. In 1839 there were two golden eagle nests and two white-tailed eagle nests – all robbed. In 1840 the birds shifted to inaccessible nest sites. In 1841 there were no golden eagles to be had. In 1842 both golden and white tailed eagle eggs were taken.

> In 1843 the whole island came into possession of one owner who stopped the taking of eggs in Hoy. Sadly, no eagles bred after that until 1887.

I am sure readers will find much of the above shocking. Shooting and killing wild animals for sport still goes on today – but it is still shocking. Those of us who don't imagine pleasure from killing do not understand it. Many of the 19th century collectors of eggs and bird skins were doing it under the auspices of natural history. Many of the great names – such as Darwin and Wallace – earned their place in history by bringing home collections of hundreds of thousands of specimens. Not all the birds taken in Orkney were in the name of science, however, many went simply to collectors who wanted to have the rarest examples and so the best and most valuable collections. The link did not appear to have been made between killing the rarest individuals and the decline of the popu-lations. Nature had always seemed inexhaustible.

It was a vicious, downward spiral – the lower the population, the rarer the individual became and so the imperative to collect one pushed up the price paid to suppliers. There may even have been a drive to 'get one before they are wiped out'. This may certainly be true of the great auk. The last known specimen in Orkney was killed on Papa Westray, in 1813 – for a collector. It is now in the Natural History Museum, London.

Buckley and Harvey-Brown's book was published in 1891 and cites research done by them and others as early as the 1860s. Farming in Orkney had changed very little in the centuries before that time. The clearances (in any case not widespread in Orkney) and 'improvements' had not started until the 1840s so old agricultural practices had developed very slowly. I think it fair to say that Orkney birdlife in 1840 was pretty similar to what it had been in (say) 1340 or even 840.

Orkney is a popular birdwatching holiday destination today. Apart from serious twitchers who flew in for the first UK chestnut bunting in 2015, or Orkney's first two-barred greenish warbler or Siberian accentor in 2016, there are people, like me, who just come to walk with binoculars. They may have come from London, Edinburgh, or Chipping Sodbury. They may have been looking forward to seeing a puffin, which would be a lifetime first for them.

Short-eared owl – with permission from Tim Wootton.

Such birdwatchers can go home at the end of a week of glorious weather with a list that includes: hen harrier, short-eared owl, white-tailed eagle, puffin and lots more besides. They will be thrilled – which they should be; and maybe satisfied – which, perhaps, they shouldn't be. I believe nature watchers all over the world are doing what the egg collectors of the 19th century were doing, they are putting a premium on rarity. Instead of being satisfied with seeing a puffin, visitors should be complaining they didn't see more. They should be asking about acidification of the ocean, loss of sand eel stocks, warming of the water, plastics and everything else leading to declining bird populations

Even insects, which prop up all our food chains, are under serious threat. When was the last time you had to clean squashed bugs off your car windscreen for instance, once a daily occurrence in summer? If insects go down then we all go down. What are we doing to our planet?

CHAPTER FORTY-ONE

# Fish Farming

I HOPE YOU will remember my description of the working landscape from earlier in the book. I view fish farms as part of that. Of
course I would rather they weren't there. I wish there was a massive, sustainable and easily accessible fish stock in the sea. I wish
there were no salmon cages just offshore on one of my favourite
walks. I wish broken bits of black pipe and nylon rope didn't
wash up on the few hundred-yards stretch of beach immediately
opposite the cages when the wind is onshore – I don't know where
they go with an offshore breeze. I wish there was no sound from
the boats and generators that operate the farm.

Looking at it another way, the visible nylon pollution from my
local fish farm is not huge. I can usually pick it all up in one walk
past. The noise is only intermittent and the cages do not intrude
on the view from miles around. Relatively cheap salmon is produced sustainably and all year round. Employment is created.

I was staying in Mull sometime in the 1970s when my host told
me of a new fish farm that had been installed up the coast. Never
having seen one I spent my evening foot-slogging up the road to
inspect it. Now that was three hours of my life I'll never get back –
they're not much to look at, just circular nets sticking up a metre
or so from the sea surface. The modern ones often have a floating
shed with them and maybe a work boat moored alongside. You
may see a worker chucking food in from time to time but even
that is beginning to be automated and computer controlled from
HQ. Underwater cameras relay information back to operators in
gaming-style chairs, in front of huge screens. They can watch the
food entering the water and see how much is being eaten by the
fish. It costs in the region of £1,000 per cage per day to feed the
fish so operators are looking for zero waste. The key parameter
is conversion rate – the percentage of food mass converted to fish

body mass. Of course, it can never be 100 per cent because of the energy used by the fish in swimming about during its lifetime. Fish farm workers receive considerable bonuses based on the minimising of waste and maximising of conversion. Just as well the gaming chairs are comfy and the screens big.

Salmon farming is a relatively recent arrival in Orkney, as in the UK generally. Witness my visit in Mull. It is new in my lifetime, I don't have to visit a Neolithic archaeological dig to find traces of its origin. That means it has developed rapidly. All aspects of salmon farming – principally animal welfare and environmental impact – are better now than they were. Of course, fish welfare is not perfect and environmental impact is not zero, so we have to decide what is acceptable. Compromise is required, as it is in almost every sphere of human activity. There are those who argue for zero tolerance but most people who have ever given it any thought will sit somewhere between extremes. I went to visit some fish farmers and this is what they said. I have put industry comments in italics.

*Seventeen per cent of farmed salmon die in the cage but this is considerably lower than for other farmed species, such as seabass (60–80 per cent) and cod (90 per cent). Ninety-five per cent of wild salmon die at sea. The figure for farmed salmon is also on a par with that for dairy, beef, sheep and pig farming.* We know that nature is red in tooth and claw so there are huge mortality rates in many wild species. In many cases death may be lingering too, so can we use the argument they lived and died, painlessly, in a cage but they had a good life? Is it good enough to point out salmon compare favourably with other farmed species? If one tyrant is less horrible than another should we forgive him? The justification of salmon farming by pointing to less good scenarios elsewhere is a central plank of the industry's argument.

*In Scotland our pens are stocked at no more than 17.5 kg of fish per cubic metre of water. These are amongst the lowest stocking densities of all salmon farming countries and ensure our fish have plenty of room to shoal in clean, oxygen-rich water.* Here's another 'We're not as bad as the other guys' claim – but are they good?

A big problem in salmon farming is the control of sea lice which live as parasites on the fish. In Orkney, however, there are no sea lice because there are no wild salmon to bring them into the area, host them and pass them to the farmed fish. This is a huge stroke of good fortune to our salmon fisheries. The stress and damage to the fish, with associated lessening of value, caused by the lice are absent. Another huge saving is on the cost of chemical treatment of lice and the damage to the environment it causes.

In areas where lice are present the industry is moving towards the use of 'cleaner fish' such as wrasse, which live in the cage with the salmon and pick off the lice for their own food (much like the oxpecker birds we are all familiar with living on the backs of cattle). The wrasse provide a personal grooming service for the salmon. This does reduce reliance on chemicals but raises the issue of welfare for the cleaner fish, which the industry is *working on*.

In addition to the use of cleaner fish salmon farmers are using Thermolicer technology to remove lice. It dislodges and catches sea lice and has seen some farms reduce chemical use by almost 25 per cent. Fish are briefly exposed to water of around 30–35°C which doesn't stress the fish but kills and dislodges the lice, which are then separated in the treatment water and destroyed.

One thing that cannot be reduced is the amount of faeces produced by the fish. These tend to sink, settle and accumulate on the bottom. The cage then leaves a footprint of more or less dead ground beneath itself. This can be reduced by periodically moving the cages (costly) or leaving them empty for a time (also costly). Faeces are less of a problem below cages that have good tidal flow through them. That said, the smaller fry cannot tolerate much current so have to be kept for a time in nursery cages with less current (they're smaller fish though, so less faecal matter).

*Any waste – be it uneaten feed, fish faeces or medicines – is closely monitored by* SEPA *(Scottish Environment Protection Agency) to ensure it stays within sustainable limits that are informed by* EU *legislation.*

'Sustainable limits' does not mean zero, it means a level of environmental damage we are prepared to tolerate or which can be reversed. We are told to leave nothing but footprints and take nothing but memories or photographs. All very well but there are almost eight billion people living on Earth (rising at 1 per cent a year, 220,000 extra humans per day or 150 per minute) and this zero impact way of life hasn't pertained since the hunter/gatherers over 5,000 years ago – and even then they would probably have argued they were sustainable rather than zero impact. 'Not as bad as those Neolithic farmers that have just moved in across the valley,' they may have said.

Wild salmon stocks have declined dramatically since the 1950s and salmon farmers have been blamed for this in certain quarters. *However: Marine Scotland data highlights that wild fish stocks have declined much more significantly on Scotland's east coast where there are no salmon farms. Causes for the decline are complex. Predators, hydro-energy, forestry and agriculture are possible contributory factors. Research is ongoing.*

And finally, salmon farmers are accused of needlessly killing seals. *Only as a last resort, should an individual seal persist beyond all preventative measures, would it be killed and then only in accordance with Marine Scotland regulations.*

Make of all that what you will.

CHAPTER FORTY-TWO

# Living by the Sea

ORCADIANS LIVE BY the sea. Only one parish in the county – Harray – has no coastline. If Harray folk want to see the ocean they have to drive a couple of miles, although Harray Loch is so big it feels a bit like the sea. Living by the sea, and with many of them working on it or by it, they have an acute awareness of all its mysteries, moods and threats. They respect the sea as only a seafaring community can. Orkney has provided seafarers for seaborne trade for centuries. They went to the whaling, exploration, the fishing, the Royal Navy and the merchant navy. Orcadian sailors have been much sought after for centuries for their knowledge of the sea and ships.

Orkney has three RNLI all-weather lifeboats, each with a volunteer crew who will drop everything when the pager sounds and go to help whoever needs them. Orcadians are fiercely proud of their lifeboat crews and they support them in every way they can with raffles, sales, fairs, dinners, fish suppers and anything else they can think of to raise funds. When the boats go out many people follow their progress on the AIS (Automatic Identification System) and do not rest until the crew is safe home. The lifeboats are close at hand. We see them every day – big, bright, orange and blue – bobbing by their pontoons in the harbours of Kirkwall, Stromness and Longhope. They are part of this special way of life too.

Perhaps nothing speaks to the heart of the Orkney way of life more than the lifeboat service. The three crews (Kirkwall, Stromness and Longhope) are almost entirely volunteers but, unlike many crews around the British Isles coast, they are almost all people who also make their livings at sea. Since 2019, I have been privileged to serve as press officer for Stromness lifeboat and have spoken in depth to some men who have spent their whole lives at sea and many years on the crew of the lifeboat. They go to sea as naturally as you and I breathe in and out. They do not see anything remarkable in it. 'We're not heroes,' they say, 'it's just what we do.' It took me a while to realise this is not modesty, false or otherwise, it really is 'just what they do'. It is a genuine and important part of their way of life, as is the love and support they get from the entire community.

CHAPTER FORTY-THREE

# The Longhope Lifeboat
# Tragedy

ON THE NIGHT of 17 March 1969, the Longhope lifeboat, *TGB*, answered a call for help from MV *Irene*, in difficulty off Orkney. A south-easterly gale had been blowing for weeks and, on her way to the casualty, *TGB* was swamped by a huge wave, with the loss of the entire crew of eight men.

*TGB* had launched, in traditional RNLI fashion, down the slip-way from the shed in the tiny community of Brims, a straggle of houses, along a single-track road on the Orkney island of Hoy. The peninsular of Brims Ness sticks down into the Pentland

The old Longhope lifeboat shed now a museum, Brims, South Walls.

Firth, one of the most dangerous stretches of water in the world. The lifeboat crew lived at Brims and not a single house was unaffected by the tragedy. Fathers, sons, brothers, husbands, friends and neighbours were lost.

Eric McFadyen had only gone down to the shed to see what was happening – after the maroons went up. Dan Kirkpatrick, the coxswain, asked him to go along. Eric climbed up the side of the boat and a life jacket was thrown to him.

Kevin Kirkpatrick – today's coxswain – lost his father (Jack), uncle (Ray) and grandfather (Dan). Kevin was not quite three years old. Kevin's wife, Karen (neé Johnston), also lost her father (Robbie), uncle (Jimmy) and grandfather (Bob). Karen had just turned two. Eric McFadyen left his mother, Chrissie, and brother Ian. Jimmy Swanson left brothers and sisters and his wife Jean. Jimmy's sister, Margaret, is 92 and remembers her big brother, Jimmy, with deep affection.

In the immediate aftermath of the tragedy there was no ready-formed crew to carry on. They only ever had a regular crew and a handful of others who would step in if needed. There was never any suggestion that the station would close however. Within a week, even before the funerals, men had come forward to be trained. The *Hilton Briggs* was stationed at Longhope and Jack Leslie from Stromness appointed as coxswain. Her first call was in June 1970. A permanent replacement – *David and Elizabeth King & EB*, with Jack Leslie as coxswain – was on station by December.

Stewart Taylor, now serving as Lifeboat Operations Manager at Stromness nearby, was just 20, and shore crew for TGB in 1969, he had worked with Dan only that morning. Stewart joined the new crew. 'There is no way of expressing it,' he said. 'We didn't replace Dan, and the others, they were irreplaceable, we just took over the roles. This was the lifeboat after all, we just had to get on with it.'

In 2018, I paid a visit to the old shed at Brims – now a lovely museum. Another old Longhope lifeboat, the Watson class, *Thomas McCunn*, is housed there. She can still shoot down the slipway, on special occasions, as she will in March to remember TGB. One corner of the museum is given over to the TGB, it contains black and white photographs, a few recovered objects and faded telegrams from The Queen and Queen Mother – telling of their deep sorrow.

The museum was attended that day by a slight young woman in a blue boiler suit. She had a rag in one hand and a tin of brass polish in the other. She introduced herself as Stella Kirkpatrick. 'Yes,' she said, 'Dan was my great grandfather, Jack and Robbie were my grandfathers. My dad has been coxswain since 2002. I'll be joining dad, and my brother Jack, on the crew next month when I turn 17.'

In March 2019, there was a commemoration in Brims for the crew of the *TGB*. Their names were read out. There were prayers and specially written music. Lifeboats and crews gathered from around Orkney and Caithness. The men of *TGB* were remembered, as they are every day round here, and we marvelled, once again, at how the RNLI continues to find such remarkable men and women who will go to those in peril on the sea.

### The Crew of The *TGB*

James (Jimmy) Johnston (34) – Second Coxswain.

Robert (Bob) Johnston (62) – Mechanic.

Robert (Robbie) Johnston (31) – Crewman.

Daniel (Dan) Kirkpatrick BEM (59) – Coxswain.

John (Jack) Kirkpatrick (26) – Crewman.

Raymond (Ray) Kirkpatrick (28) – Bowman.

Eric McFadyen (24) – Crewman.

James (Jimmy) Swanson (61) – Assistant Mechanic.

The Longhope lifeboat memorial, South Walls.

CHAPTER FORTY-FOUR

# The Stromness Lifeboat

THE *VIOLET, DOROTHY and Kathleen,* stationed at Stromness since 1998, is a Severn class, all-weather lifeboat (ALB). The other ALB types in the fleet are Tyne, Mersey, Trent and Tamar. They are all self-righting and are fitted with navigation, location and communication equipment of the highest standards. Each boat has a working life of about 25 years.

Developed by the RNLI in the early 1990s, the Severn class lifeboat is designed to lie afloat and is inherently self-righting. The propellers and rudder lie in partial tunnels set into the hull that, along with two bilge keels, provide excellent protection in shallow water. The Severn carries an additional, inflatable daughter boat with a 5hp outboard engine and capable of 6 knots. She is used to access areas the bigger boat cannot go. The comprehensive electronics include VHF and MF radios with DSC functionality, VHF direction finder, DGPS with electronic chart system and radar. First aid equipment includes stretchers, oxygen and Entonox. There is also a portable salvage pump carried in a watertight container.

In return for their dedication and commitment, the RNLI makes a pledge to its volunteer crew that the boat and equipment is maintained to the highest standards and able to respond to emergencies at sea. There is a regular and extensive refit process which sees the entire craft stripped and rebuilt as needed.

Since March 2019 it has been my privilege to be press officer for Stromness lifeboat station so I thought it would be nice for local folk to know a bit about members of their crew, and what they get up to when they're out on a shout. I sat down with one or two of them in the station one day and heard a few of the stories:

Fred Breck was coxswain of the Stromness lifeboat when I arrived in Orkney in 2017. I well remember him plucking a wallflower (Bev) to dance strip the willow at the RNLI dance in our first week here. Her husband, being a miserable, stiff old bugger had declined her invitations. Fred started his career at sea as crewman in a fishing boat for Alfie Sinclair of Stromness. At that time Alfie was coxswain of the Stromness boat, it was 1970 and the boat on station was an old Barnett class. They had just finished fishing for the week and were sorting out their boat in the harbour when the maroons went off. Fred was recruited to the crew and he rode down the slipway with Alfie and the others in true lifeboat tradition.

A number of years at sea followed before Fred came ashore to work at the navigation school in Stromness. By 1998, the station had the Arun class boat and Fred was appointed second coxswain. In 2004 he represented the Stromness lifeboat station at the opening, by her Majesty the Queen, of the new Lifeboat College in Poole. A year later Fred was made coxswain.

When asked which of his many shouts (lifeboat jargon for a callout or service), he would remember most vividly when he finally retires. His first answer concerned a comedy moment with nothing of the heroism or drama one associates with the lifeboat:

> We got a call from a farmer at Warbeth, overlooking Hoy Sound, just round the corner from Stromness. One of his calves had decided to swim out to sea. We couldn't get close enough with the big boat so we launched the inflatable off the stern and two crew members went and rescued the calf. When they got it back to the big boat we all wanted to know if either of them had needed to give it the kiss of life.

Fred then went on to talk about the tragedies of recovering the bodies of suicide victims. The high cliff at Yesnaby, on Orkney Mainland's west coast, is a notorious spot. When someone goes over, sometimes accidentally, there is little hope for them and the only way of recovering the body is from the lifeboat. This is a part of the service Fred clearly does not relish.

Fred still hadn't mentioned a dramatic shout but then said:

> We got a call one winter afternoon just as it was getting
> dark, a man on his own had gone out in a small yole
> from Birsay to attend to his creels. When he didn't come
> back for tea his wife raised the alarm and we launched
> the boat. We passed out of Hoy sound and turned north
> under the cliffs of West Mainland heading for Birsay. The
> light was failing and the wind was freshening from the
> south, we could tell that the sea off Birsay was no place to
> be in a small yole. We lit the searchlight and commenced
> sweeping the area. Back and forth we went for a good
> while. If the fishing boats engine had failed he would be
> drifting northwards all the time so we gradually moved
> our search pattern to take account of this. Eventually, at
> about 8 o'clock, we found Jimmy standing in his boat
> waving an oar in the air. Jimmy was mightily relieved
> when he stepped onto the lifeboat. We tried to tow his
> boat home but in the worsening weather it was swamped
> and lost – I think Jimmy was relieved all over again that
> it was gone.

This was not a dramatic, heroic rescue. The lifeboat was never in
any danger and in many ways it was a simple search operation. It
would hardly make an episode in an adventure film. I think Fred
chose it because it illustrated the quiet determination to be of service to fellow seafarers.

> We would have gone on looking all night. After daybreak
> we would almost certainly have found him or, in the worst
> case, learned what had happened to him.'

Jimmy Norquoy was happy to tell his version of events on that
(almost) fateful night.

> It was 4 September, I mind it because it was my wed-
> ding anniversary. I had just come home on leave that day
> and my outboard motor was waiting for me having been
> away to be serviced. It was not a very bonny night but

I wanted to try the motor so I thought I would just go to a few creels.

I collected those that were close inshore, in Skipi Geo, and then thought ach it's no so bad, I'll go a bit further. This was when the engine stopped, the wind and waves were kicking up and I started to drift. I threw the creels back in to give me a bit of an anchor, it was impossible to row against the wind, the oars just kept lifting out of the ro'locks. My son, John, had not been keen to come out with me because of the weather but luckily he was keeping an eye from the shore and could see I was struggling. He called my wife, Greer, and between them they decided to call the coastguard, who alerted the lifeboat in Stromness. I didn't feel too worried at this point, I didn't feel in immediate danger and I knew I'd been seen so I kept on trying to start the engine. Eventually it started so I cast off the creels and headed for shore – big mistake – the engine only ran for a few seconds before cutting out again. Now I was drifting and couldn't reach the creels to anchor myself again.

The current was taking me towards some skerries over which quite a lot of water was breaking, I knew I had to use the oars to steady the boat and try to avoid the skerry. I tried my anchor but the cable was too short and it dragged. I was still drifting. There was far too much swell breaking on the rocks and cliffs for me to attempt putting into shore. Then at last I saw the lifeboat, it was fully dark by now but I could see her searchlight. She was too far out, going up and down, and I couldn't understand why she wasn't finding me, why aren't I on the radar I thought. Low and behold the engine started again and I decided to head out for the lifeboat. This was not good, it only ran for 20 seconds again, just enough time to deposit me in the full fury of the wind and tide but not enough for me to reach the lifeboat. My wee boat started to take water and I had just about given up, I took the oars into the boat and more or less waited for the end. I cannot swim and have always had a morbid fear of drowning. By this time I had drifted right round the north end and could see down into Eynhallow Sound.

Then, all at once, she was there. The Stromness Lifeboat was alongside my peedie yole – Puffin. They tell me I had been standing up and waving an oar in the air, whatever, they found me. I stepped onto the lifeboat and the boys took the yole in tow.

At this point Fred and Jimmy agree absolutely on a detail of the story:

Jimmy: I had never been so relieved in my life.

Fred: That was one very relieved man when he stepped on board the lifeboat.

We set off back to Stromness with the yole in tow but she was swamped by the wash from the boat. Fred asked me what I wanted to do but I wasn't in a fit state to worry about the yole so I just told them to let it go. It will have drifted away and broken up somewhere.

(Bits of it were found on Westray a few days later.) Incidentally, the company that serviced the engine was still demanding payment. It was pointed out that, because a man had almost lost his life as a result of their engine, they would not be getting paid. Nothing further was heard on this matter. Jimmy said:

Now that the emergency was over, people onshore piled into a house, where copious volumes of soup had been prepared (our neighbour always prepares soup in a crisis) this was enjoyed by all the coastguards and others who had turned out to help.

My daughter-in-law, Kristen, drove down to Stromness and collected me from the lifeboat steps and brought me home. We never did celebrate our wedding anniversary.

Jimmy wasn't carrying any flares or even a torch and certainly not a radio when he set out to his creels. Fred Breck did not tell me that until I asked. He clearly knew Jimmy had made a mistake but was not interested in looking for someone to blame, he was just pleased to have been of service. Jimmy, on the other hand, couldn't stop telling me how embarrassed he felt at being so careless and especially at having to call out the lifeboat.

When all is said and done the men and women who go to sea in our lifeboats are all people who live and work by, or on, the sea. They all understand the pull of the sea and the need many of us have to be on it, sometimes in poor weather and, occasionally, ill-equipped. They recognise that mistakes will be made and do not punish us too harshly when we make them. They will turn out when we need them and, as Fred said, they will search all night if they have to. A final thought on this story – at the point where Jimmy's engine started for the last time, and took him out into real danger, the lifeboat crew were having a discussion about whether to go further out or continue the search nearer to shore. They decided to come in – and that made all the difference.

I asked Fred if there had ever been an occasion when the weather was simply too bad for the lifeboat to go. He told me of one shout when they were called to assist a boat apparently in difficulties somewhere to the west.

> The coastguard was picking up an EPIRB signal [Emergency Position Indication Radio Beacon, designed to send a signal, via satellite, to the coastguard when a ship is in distress. The signal is coded and includes the name of the boat. It can either be manually activated or by contact with water]. The trouble was the signal was jumping about all over the place. One minute it was coming from Cape Wrath 70 miles away, the next it was close to Orkney. We got to the mouth of the harbour and Hoy Sound was boiling. Gale force wind going against the tide and all trying to go through the narrow channel. Hell's Mouth some people call it. I asked the coastguard if they could absolutely

confirm there was someone out there in need of us. They decided the signal was so erratic they would not know where to direct us so we stood down.

It was eventually established that the boat in question had been sold to an Orkney man who had changed its name and taken the EPIRB off. The EPIRB unit was sitting in a bucket in a shed at Stromness. Somehow water had got to it and set it off.

Stewart Taylor is Lifeboat Operations Manager at Stromness. He said:

Having been born and brought up close to the Longhope Lifeboat Station it was always my ambition to become part of the crew. My grandfather, father, uncles and cousins were all involved one way or another. I first started as a shore helper at the age of 14 and then joined the crew in 1969 after the Longhope disaster (the entire crew of eight were lost when the Longhope boat – TGB – was swamped by a freak wave whilst out on service on 17th March 1969). In 1971, wanting to be more involved with the boat, I became a reserve mechanic. My duties included relieving station mechanics, delivering lifeboats to and from boatyards and assisting on boat refits. When I was offered the position of Stromness station mechanic I quickly accepted and remained in that post for 31 years, up to the (then) compulsory retirement age of 55.

Lifeboats changed a lot during my service, from the 8 knot, 140hp Barnett type to an 18 knot, 1,000hp Arun and, finally, the 25 knot, 2,500hp Severn we have today. Administration has changed too, from log books to computers.

The slipway and boathouse in Dundas Street are also things of the past, with the present boat having an afloat berth within the harbour and a workshop / changing room on the pier, adjacent to the new station.

'Shouts' vary greatly, from saving a calf from the sea to towing a replica galley 70 miles from Cape Wrath to Stromness. Diving incidents increased as Scapa Flow became popular with recreational divers visiting the scuttled German fleet. I was delighted to be invited, on my retirement, to join the station management group and become a deputy launching authority. It keeps me in contact with the RNLI and, in particular the crew who I miss working alongside.

In 2010, after the untimely death of William (Rothes) Duncan, Stewart was appointed Lifeboat Operations Manager – back in harness once again.

CHAPTER FORTY-FIVE

# A Fair Breeze o' Wind

THE ROYAL NATIONAL Lifeboat Institution is the charity that saves lives at sea, founded in 1824 and with a boat based at Stromness by 1867. There has been a continuous presence here ever since. In 2017, the RNLI Stromness Lifeboat Station celebrated its 150th anniversary.

The RNLI is a magnificent organisation. There can be few higher ideals than that of saving the life, without asking for anything in return, of anyone in peril on the sea regardless of race, colour or creed. The volunteer crew members – all 5,500 of them around our coast – will put down their knives and forks at Christmas lunch, turn out of bed at 3.00am or simply drop a good book and put to sea, often in weather that has others heading for harbour, all because the pager has sounded and they know someone needs them. Lifeboat crews do not consider themselves heroes, but I am not a crew member so I don't have to hold back. They *are* our real, live, genuine heroes and they should know just how much they are loved and appreciated.

John Davidson might be one of the most familiar to locals. He is the only full-time crew member in Stromness and is employed by the RNLI as mechanic. You will often see him in his navy blue RNLI boiler suit around the boat or the station

John is an Orcadian, born and raised in Stromness before joining the Royal Navy aged 16. John served a lot of his 24 years in the navy on fisheries protection vessels based at Rosyth. In October 1989 he found himself in HMS *Orkney* when she attended the 50th anniversary of the sinking of HMS *Royal Oak* in Scapa Flow. As the youngest member of the crew, and an Orkneyman, John was given the honour of laying a wreath alongside the Flag Officer. On 14 October 2019, he was again at *Royal Oak* for

the 80th anniversary to lay petals on the sea in his capacity as
Chair of Stromness British Legion. Navy people always remember their own and John has been very proud to perform these
tasks on behalf of the people of Orkney, who themselves will hold
the memory of the men and boys of *Royal Oak* in safe keeping
for ever.

After his service in the Navy, John came home to Stromness
and joined the crew as mechanic in 2011. I asked him what had
been the most memorable shout and he immediately recalled a
Spanish fishing vessel, struggling in heavy seas out west. A huge
wave had smashed in the wheelhouse window resulting in the loss
of engine power and electronics. Luckily the radio still worked.
By the time *Violet Dorothy and Kathleen* arrived, they had managed to restore the engine but navigation was still a problem so
they followed the lifeboat to Westray. 'No sooner had we got there
the coastguard asked us if we would take a man to Kirkwall as
his wife was in labour and all transport was shut by the gale,'
John said.

When pressed for his funniest memories, he said:

> We always have a smile when it's one of our crew that needs
> a tow home. We have a chart in the shed with a blue pin for
> each of the places we've been. Our own crew members get
> a red pin.

> Whenever I head out from Stromness marina in my own
> small boat, I double check my equipment carefully. I would
> hate to find myself bobbing about in Scapa Flow with
> engine failure and have to call the coastguard. I do not want
> the lifeboat to be called out on my account and be peer-
> ing up at yellow-clad, smiling faces looking down from the
> rail and someone saying, 'Oh, it's you.' I don't know if I'd
> qualify for a red pin but, blue or red, it would still be an
> embarrassment.

> Sometimes, of course, it is much more than embarrassment at
> stake. Fred Breck, recently retired coxswain, told me a while
> ago about pulling a man from a tiny boat drifting out to sea

in the dark: 'That was one very relieved man when he stepped on board the lifeboat,' said Fred. 'I had given up, I thought my time had come,' said the man, 'and then, suddenly, the lifeboat was right there beside me. I have never been so relieved in my life.'

Colin Mowat is coxswain of the Stromness lifeboat today. His lifeboat career, however, extends back to childhood when he would muster at the old 'red shed' lifeboat station in Shopping Week to ride, with as many of his pals as could be squeezed aboard, when the boat went down the slipway purely for their benefit. Sadly, the treat has been consigned to the pages of history by Health & Safety.

Colin went to sea, aged just 16 (and during school holidays before that) with his uncle, Willie Sinclair, to work on MV *Merlin II* at the crab and lobster inshore fishing. He joined the lifeboat crew soon after but in those days RNLI was not the organisation it has become. There was no 'strength in depth' to the crew. Most launches were attended by the same five or six men who had been doing it for years. It was quite some time before Colin's turn came. Today there are about 20 on the Stromness crew and all can expect to be trained to a very high standard and needed from time to time.

Gradually the training on such things as navigation, first aid and sea survival took greater prominence and qualified Colin to take the helm as coxswain. 'We had to go in a wave tank at Aberdeen,' he said. 'That was no picnic. We were in a dingy, in huge waves, in the dark, with the sound of a helicopter right above our heads and water being sprayed from all sides. It turned our stomachs but was good training.'

One of Colin's most memorable shouts was to another fishing boat out to the west of Orkney. 'The wind picked up as we steamed out and it was force eight or nine when we got to the casualty. We took her in tow and made for Scrabster but the line parted about six times. We had another but that parted too. In the end the Thurso boat had to come out and between us we got her to Scrabster pier. Aye there was a fair breeze o' wind that night.'

Norman Brass runs a garage in Stromness. Although one of
the few crew members based on shore he has lived and worked
close to the sea all his life. An early memory is of rowing down
the harbour to primary school (aged about 10) in his own peedie
boat from his home at the south end. He and his dad soon clubbed
together for a 1.5 HP outboard and he has been boat and engine
mad ever since (Currently up to 2 x 220 HP). Norman is a relief
coxswain/mechanic who could, in theory, volunteer for relief
duties at other stations but work stays him in Stromness mostly.

Norman remembers the night before the service to the
Spanish boat:

> I was just going to bed. I turned out the light and stood for
> a moment to let my eyes adapt to the dark. The gale had
> whipped up a wall of water all the way across Hoy Sound.
> I remember thinking we'll no be called out the night, there'll
> be nobody out there. But by 6.00am the pagers had gone off
> and Colin had found us the only possible way out through
> the breakers, close to the Graemsay shore. By 9.00pm the
> next night we had circumnavigated Orkney Mainland in a
> gale, escorted a fishing boat to safety, taken a man to his
> wife in labour and managed to grab a bite to eat in Kirkwall
> on the way home. Three deliveries that day.

I'll give the last word (almost) to Lifeboat Operations Manager,
Stuart Taylor, who has been with the crew longer than he cares
to remember:

> It was in the days of the old slipway launches and we were
> called out in the middle of the night. We only had five men
> and needed someone on shore to release the boat. Stella had
> her bedroom immediately above the shed so I called up to
> her to put on boots and a mac over her nightie and come
> down as we needed her. Stella's reply was colourful but the
> gist was that under no circumstance was she going in the
> boat. Assured that would not be necessary she came down.
> Do you think you can give that pin a mighty blow with this
> hammer Stella? I asked. 'Of course,' she said, and with that
> took the hammer and clouted the pin before I'd time to climb

on board. The boat slid into the harbour leaving me high and dry and standing beside Stella in her boots and mac. The boat circled round, came back for me and off we went.

Absolutely finally, I bumped into Coreen Mowat, Colin's wife, doing a shift of Christmas card selling in the RNLI Stromness gift shop next door to the lifeboat station. 'Things are much better now we have the AIS,'[1] she said. 'We all still worry of course, when the pagers go off in the middle of the night – it always seems to be the middle of the night with a gale blowing – when they have to pull on their clothes and go. I always get up. I can't sleep any more at that point so I make a cup of tea and potter about. I put the AIS on the computer and that tells me where the boat is and which way they're headed. Will it be left out of Hoy Sound and south towards Scrabster? Or will they turn right and head out into the western sea? The screen tells me when they start heading back. I might be able to see from the speed if they're towing something. No matter, it's a relief when they're all safe home.'

---

1 AIS = Automatic Identification System. Transponders on vessels are identified by satellites and can be located and followed, in real time, by anyone with a smart phone or computer.

CHAPTER FORTY-SIX

# A Survivor's Daughter Remembers

KATHY KIRK, FROM near Hull, got in touch one day to ask if she could have a Stromness RNLI pin badge. I asked what her particular interest in Stromness lifeboat was and she agreed to let me reproduce the whole story. 'I'll write down everything I can remember,' she said.

> I was 13 years old and at home with my brothers and sisters on the evening of 25 January 1965. My mam had gone to the bingo, a rare treat for a mother of eight, so my elder sister was babysitting.
>
> The television news announced the loss of the *Kingston Turquoise*, a Hull trawler. My dad, John (Jock) Neilson, was Bo'sun on the *Turquoise*! Luckily, mam came home just after, and I remember frantic phone calls. She managed to get numbers for exotic-sounding places like Wick and Stromness. We finally heard that most of the crew were safe, my dad included. We all just sat and cried with relief.
>
> Eventually, Dad arrived home in Hull, wearing clothes the good people of Stromness had provided, as they had only what they were wearing when she went down. It had been so fast, just four minutes, no one had been able to save anything.
>
> Dad told us how the Stromness lifeboat had launched, and, despite weather conditions being appalling, had not given up in their search for the men, and had, after many hours in terrible seas, managed to locate the life rafts.
>
> Dad was very affected by the loss of his shipmate, Walter Danton, who had, after helping launch the life rafts, gone

back to his cabin for his dog. The seas had wrenched the rafts away from the trawler, and the heavy conditions meant they were unable to reach Walter, even though they were not that far away from him. He said how they had to listened to him shouting, 'over here, lads, please be quick' whilst trying to reach him, but after a very short time, they couldn't hear him anymore.

Because of the heroism (yes, *real* heroism, in the true sense of the word) of the crew of the lifeboat and of the Shackleton aircraft which eventually guided the lifeboat to the rafts by dropping flares, we were able to enjoy a further 30 years with my Dad, who died on the 5th January 1996.

When my mam died, on 14 January 2014, she left a legacy for Stromness lifeboat station. The money donated at her funeral was paid to the national RNLI.

In 2015 (almost exactly 50 years after the rescue), my husband and I visited Stromness to be greeted by crew man David Bowdler who showed us round the station and the lifeboat. David introduced us to Operations Manager Stewart Taylor (too young to be crew in 1965 but who was involved on the shore) and, incredibly, to Willie Sinclair who had been part of the rescue. I cannot possibly describe the emotions of that meeting.

We went along to the old lifeboat station to see the wooden plaques on display, showing the dates and names of the rescues performed by the Stromness crews through the years. And of course, the *Kingston Turquoise* was up there. Incredible. All those lives saved by men who didn't have to put to sea, gained nothing materially, but went anyway.

A day I will never, ever forget. I have been to Stromness, and nothing can take away those wonderful memories.

Willie is 85 and still goes to the creels in his boat, *Merlin II*, most days when weather allows. He says he feels much better when he works. He left school and joined the lifeboat at 14. The boat was going on a shout up to Lashy Sound, Sanday and the coxswain asked him if he fancied a trip. Today the Kirkwall lifeboat would take that call but there was no lifeboat there until 1968. Furthermore, the lifeboat would not take an untried, untrained 14-year-old boy, without parental permission today – but this was 1948, not 2020. Willie eventually became 2nd mechanic and did seven years as coxswain until he retired aged 56 in 1990. Willie was on the boat, the Barnett class *Archibald and Alexander M Patterson*, the night of the service to *Kingston Turquoise*. I asked him to tell me what he remembered of the rescue:

> There was a fair breeze from the NE that night. There were a lot of boats out searching [trawlers from Hull, Grimsby and Aberdeen on their way back from Iceland after poor fishing there]. The track from Iceland to Orkney takes them directly over the North Shoal, even so, they were unlucky to hit it, hid's no very big. The man lost [Walter Denton] had been torpedoed twice during the war and survived. He helped organise the two rafts with half the men in each. He recovered his dog – Lassie – who was in one of the rafts but they were torn away from the ship before he could get in. Lassie jumped out of the raft to swim to him and they were both lost.
>
> The RAF Shackleton found the rafts and someone on a raft put up a flare. The Shackleton radioed the position to the lifeboat, which happened to be the nearest vessel to the rafts. We picked up all 19 men in the rafts uninjured and brought them back to Stromness.
>
> They were put up in the Temperance Hotel [now the Ferry Inn].

### Would you like to help?

The RNLI is glamorous, it has 431 lifeboats, including 160 of the big all-weather lifeboats that we love to see doing 25 knots and breasting huge seas in their shiny blue and orange livery. They cost over £2 million each so be under no illusion, running the fleet is a very expensive business, paid for entirely from voluntary donations. The RNLI is a charity and receives absolutely no government funding.

If you'd like to support the volunteer crews of the RNLI there are plenty of collecting boxes around Orkney and almost every town and city in the UK has collecting days and events of one sort or another. You could also drop into any lifeboat station to see what you could do; they'd be very pleased to see you.

Stromness lifeboat – *Violet Dorothy and Kathleen.*

# Part Four – Conclusions, Looking Back and Looking Forward

CHAPTER FORTY-SEVEN

# Writing by Senior Students at Kirkwall Grammar School

FOR MY LAST book, *Orkney – A Special Place*, I visited Kirkwall Grammar School and Westray Junior High School to talk to the students about their feelings for Orkney. They produced some excellent writing on the subject which I included, more or less unedited, in the book. Readers reported enjoying the work so I've been back to Kirkwall for more.

### Cruise liners

I glance outside, through the strangers I recognise a familiar face, where pale, bare arms swing from side to side, standing out amongst the jackets and scarves worn by visitors. I smile and give a small nod as they return a grin and then return to weaving through the bustling crowd. The shop is shut and it's still light outside, a fresh, cool breeze catches my hair. I make my way up the streets I could find in my sleep, past the shops, castle and Cathedral, still standing. The town is now quiet. I turn around to catch the cruise liner on its way to the next destination. A giant compared to the ferries transporting locals to the northern isles. I inhale the crisp air and breathe a sigh of relief.

## The cathedral

The cracks in the paved streets, a map known like the back of my hand, pointing to the main attraction. The red sandstone building that looms over the town, constantly watching. Its neighbour a palace slowly crumbling. The gravestones across the road hidden beside the Cathedral, broken, engraved with the names of those who once walked the Orkney soil. They all hold their own history, unspoken and unknown.

ALLANAH LOUTTIT

## Orkney dialect

'Hi aye buey, what like the day?' 'No bad, whit like yourself?' is a typical greeting conversation you might overhear in the local pubs, supermarkets or even just on the main streets of Orkney. Orkney would not be Orkney without its dialect. It makes us Orcadians who we are today. To us Orcadians, our slang is just a part of who we are, but go outside of Orkney and speak the dialect, I can tell you, you'll get a lot of strange looks.

The Orcadian dialect comes from old Norse language and words often referred to as Norn. When the dialect originated it was originally known as the 'speech of the ignorant'. The dialect is no longer known as that nowadays. The dialect used to be deliberately suppressed in schools but thankfully that is now no longer the case. Place names are now pronounced wrongly too and many words have been forgotten. It's a shame to see Orcadian dialect deteriorating because it's a part of Orkney.

RHEA LAUGHTON

## Growing up in Orkney

When asked about growing up in Orkney, many things come to mind.

Firstly, I think of the freedom. Long summer nights spent under orange skies, finding my own way home in the early hours of the morning. Making my way through the town, through the peaceful lanes and roads which I know inside out. Saturday evening, the harbour, pubs and bars are bustling, familiar drunks call to me in greeting which I laugh about the rest of the way home. Windows and doors are permanently unlocked. No matter where you are, who you're with or what you're doing, the spire of the St Magnus Cathedral will be watching over you.

However, I visited my sister in Glasgow and I noticed. I noticed she locked the door to her flat when we went for lunch. I noticed that nobody smiled or nodded at us as we passed them on the street. We didn't laugh when the drunk men called to us as we passed a bar and I realised.

I realised that growing up in Orkney has made me too naive and too trusting.

But I don't care. It has set a standard for how people all over the world should treat each other.

IZZY NICHOLSON

---

It's hard to imagine

It's hard to imagine life away from Orkney. It has truly been a great place to live in the short 17 years I've been here and I wouldn't have wanted to grow up anywhere else. I'm never far away from a friendly face, eye catching culture or the fresh salt water sea, which makes everyday a breath of fresh air – literally. However, I feel like it's time for a change, something different. It's coming to the time where I may have the chance to leave Orkney, to take the next step on the life ladder.

Orkney is a very friendly place. Doors are left unlocked, children play out till dark – sometimes after – and everybody knows everybody, which has its pros and cons. If I do leave Orkney, getting to know new faces and meet different people will be something I look forward to. Don't get me wrong, I have made many great friends here in Orkney, but there is a sense of people knowing more about my business than I do – which I'm sure happens in any small community. I'm really hoping that a city could change that. Every time I've been to a city further afield, I've had a tremendous time! Magnificent glass structures imprisoning me into spending my limited amount of cash; walking down the beautifully crafted cobble stone pathways as I breath in the fresh, soupy smog; jumping on the well-paced, fast-paced trams, only to be jam-packed like a sardine next to the late mums and angry business men with their bulky briefcases and tumultuous phone calls. Is it so great after all?

Even if I leave Orkney, I think I will always come back: I can't see it being a permanent move. The whole city lifestyle seems to me like an overly hyped novelty. It's a break from Orkney life, not a replacement. I couldn't stay away from those friendly faces forever.'

JAMIE CLOUSTON

---

## What do you see?

When I say the word 'Orkney', what do you see? An array of Neolithic settlements; a ring of high stones, some fallen and weathered with age; a Romanesque cathedral of pinks and reds. Places the visitor brochures will never fail to mention, repeated year after year. But when I say the word 'Orkney', what do you *hear*?

In late May each year, the Orkney Folk festival fills the cobbled streets of Stromness with ditties, jigs and reels. Musicians from Shetland, the Western Isles, America and Canada grace the Island's stages. I have seen unknown, unpronounceable instruments come from unheard of countries. Once, I saw a man tap dance on top of his double bass.

I have sung and played in the festival from the age of 13. I remember performing in an attempted recreation of the Edinburgh Military Tattoo three years ago: a cheesy, show-off display of dancing while playing the fiddle. Personally, I find dancing a reel hard enough already without my arms being inconvenienced with an instrument. While I do enjoy the multiculturalism of the festival, I did not enjoy this.

But after four years of performing, what I love most are the more 'local' gigs. Far removed from the pretentiousness of a tattoo, are little concerts in village halls. These small gatherings will not promise anything extravagant or showy, but rather good, unadulterated music and kind hospitality.

Among my happiest memories of the festival is the time I and my group performed in the community centre on the island of Shapinsay. I remember being greeted and welcomed by the ladies of the island who fed us before we had even played. They seemed happy to have us and were genuinely interested in a group of young fiddle players as they walked in between the tables, stopping to chat and offering us more of their delicious soup. The lovely thing about concerts like these is that the mostly Orcadian audience will already know the tunes we play. Elderly ladies' heads will sway, and their lips will mouth the words of 'The fair Orkney Islands' or 'The Orkney Anthem'. Sometimes I hear them humming quietly to themselves, or sometimes just quietly smiling.

Being an incomer to Orkney, I am incredibly thankful for the audiences of local citizens. A few years ago, I attended the Orkney county show with one of my friends. An Orcadian friend. A constant stream of 'hello's left her mouth as every few seconds she would have to interrupt our conversation to greet yet another one of her family members. 'That was my uncle', 'my cousin', or 'my other uncle', she would explain to me after they had passed. I was envious of her. She had family members around her in abundance and she would always have someone to say hello to. Yet I soon realised that, thanks to music, I too always have someone to say hello to. I always find that a few days after a small concert, as I make my way down Broad Street, I am stopped by one of its attendees. I love seeing their faces light up in recognition of me, as they sigh and say, 'You young folk are so talented,' or 'That song you sang was right bonny.'

This is why I love the cramped tightness of a gig in a village hall. On a bigger stage, I am just a body moving with the others to create a pretty shape for frivolous entertainment. On a smaller stage, I am me – standing tall in front of a microphone, singing and playing, open and intimate with my audience who can clearly see my hair, eyes, arms and legs. A person they will recognise later. When I am complimented and congratulated for my music, I feel like I have given back to a truly remarkable place that my family chose to make their home.

SOPHIE SULLIVAN

## Back streets

Admittedly, Orkney is full of beauty on its surface. There is no denying that. There is no denying that within descriptive books and colourful brochures, Orkney is presented as the peacock among the pigeons. For the short-time visitor perhaps this is true. Truth is subjective and who am I to judge a person's perception of a place. Thou shalt not judge thy neighbour, as the Lord commanded. However, I am unsure of how close He is to this place, and whether His commandments have been able to breach the flakey persona of this place. I am still unsure how one of the smallest inhabited places could have such an impact on the lives of those who live here: the long-time unfortunates.

Seeing the reality of this island is not as hard as it may appear, one must only be first aware of where to look. And not just look. Those who know this place well know where the quiet is. While tourists, and locals who know no different to this place, flood the main road, the incomers here dive behind buildings to dash down back streets. A busy capital is not as safe as it may seem. Somehow 50 miles of ocean can cause a tidal wave of a difference between civilisation and island life.

There is pain hidden behind the beauty of the landscape.

Walk to the end of the main road and the horizon bursts into a vast spread of the ocean below the Sun that is a little too high in the sky. At night though is perhaps when this place truly comes alive. People walk up and down the strip lining the marina, intently watching the boats across the expanse of dark water interspersed with reflected lights. Reflections on the water that blind passers-by from the reality that one only sees when they know the back streets. If even one of these people walked around the small headland at one corner of the strip, they could catch a glimpse of the island's reality. Lonely faceless individuals adorned with black holes where eyes should be hide around the headland. Black holes only concerned with distracting themselves from their reality with the turning mobile of the same reflections that blind the rest of the world. Leaving them still unseen. Just trying to find an escape from the reality of the life this island brings. One cannot say what causes the abundance of this issue; whether it is boredom or a lack of care, it is impossible to say. Heathy activities come few and far between here, especially for those who are young and most vulnerable. This perhaps sparks the idea for the chance for escape, only escalated by the knowledge that those who swore to protect will turn a blind eye too.

If those passers-by where to walk in the opposite direction, they would eventually come across buildings of great history. Of course, the grand Cathedral cannot be ignored, however just across the road is the Earl's Palace. 400 years of history held in one erection of stone. Touring historians and enthusiasts alike flock here to stand in the wake of such a relic. They climb the weathered stairs to look across the capital and try to imagine what life was like when this Palace was in use. However, they do not look to the adjoining garden holding a small bench. This new addition, out of place close to a building so old. Perhaps that is why those lonely outsiders choose to take refuge here. Many a cold night the souls of those seeking some quiet, some silence, come here to try to rest. Orkney may not be a busy place, but the noise here is deafening. London provided more peace then Kirkwall. For it is not the audible noise that is deafening here, it is the environment. Every corner turned, every café frequented, every shop entered holds a history. In such a small place one cannot avoid the memories. In such a small place one cannot avoid those who gave you them. That is why this place is deafening. Every stone on the ground reminds you of a time you lost. The sounds of these memories is what creates the crushing din. That is why small areas of reprieve are so vital here, that is why these areas are little known, that is why they are not seen, because those in need of a muted world do not wish to be seen.

A little further up the main street is the natural beauty of Tankerness Gardens. During summer it could look like the sister to Claude Monet's own garden in Giverny. Flowers bloom at every turn and young parents can play with their children, enjoying this time with them knowing they will grow up in what will seem like a flash. But as always here, places that hold beauty on the surface hide the places with the most sorrow. That 50 miles of water did not seem to part to allow for the knowledge of those who are different to reach this place. The need for two boys to hide in this array of flowers all colours of the rainbow is the ironic reality of this place. They cannot be close. They cannot look for too long. They cannot touch. They cannot utter the words of given to them by our Father. Perhaps this is what shows that He is not with us here, for we cannot love our neighbour as He loves us. I cannot love him with the love He gave me. Hands break apart with the sound of footsteps threatening to discover their safe haven. Voices are hushed and body's change their language as the steps get closer, vying to expose the boys in their soft vulnerability. Hiding because one wishes to be unnoticed in the process of self-sabotage or hiding to preserve oneself from the damage of memories from a lost time is somewhat understandable despite the pain behind these actions. Hiding because those around you do not view the love he has for him as acceptable brings more pain. When love is condemned in a place, one begins to question the sanctity of all the morals there.

Orkney cannot be said to be ugly. It is beautiful. But only on the surface. Like a Medusa behind a mask, that mask will fool any man who sees it, he will move closer, trusting his attraction to it. What he does not know is the aesthetics of the mask is merely a manufactured facade to draw him in. Once he is close enough she will reveal her true nature and he will be cast to stone. Forever trapped wondering how something so attractive could harbour the ability to be the downfall of him and many others who have fallen before his time. This place will draw you in with its warm sunsets above soft beaches, rolling hills punctuated by herds of indigenous cattle and historical architecture. But once you are close enough it will reveal the Medusa found when one walks the back streets from behind this mask. Eventually you too will be cast into stone by the bad habits this place harbours and fails to combat; the inability to escape overwhelming screeds of memories; and the unholy condemnation of a love considered foreign.

One has to be prepared to not only look, but truly see what is hidden down the back streets. Then. Only then. Can one begin to understand the true nature of this island. It is not as full of grace and peace as perhaps some may encourage you to believe. Quite the opposite.

There is pain hidden behind the beauty of the landscape.

ALEX GIBSON

---

## The darkness

It wasn't a good day. Shocking. It was cloudy. It was overcast. I'm pretty sure it rained – but that wouldn't be a shock. The weather was, reliably, disappointing; although, for this, I am glad. I don't think I could have handled the sun making this day better. It wasn't a happy day... it wasn't a good day... I don't even really like the sun – not here anyway.

We went to the beach after they told us. Not all of us – they didn't come... I wouldn't have liked that. We walked there. I cried. I remember the sky was white. But it was not peaceful. Death... Mourning... Sadness... the eastern cultures had it right. It wasn't a good day – everyone should notice. I felt... broken. I don't know how long we were gone for. It didn't feel long enough. I wanted to come back whole. I didn't. I couldn't. I wouldn't. It hurt. I tried to be strong. I wasn't. But I hate crying, especially in front of people. It didn't work. It never does. Nothing was the same. I remember the lump in my throat, a painfully obvious reminder of just how fine I wasn't. My eyes stung with tears. Watering. Overflowing. Crashing down my face. I didn't know what to do. I had never thought this would happen. I had been oblivious... They thought I had seen it coming.

I hadn't.

I didn't understand. How could I not have noticed? I was angry. I was confused. I was alone. Everyone else had known... or thought... or something... I was alone. I was alone, and it hurt. I wish there had been more rain – but, even that had been disappointing. Barely noticeable. Light... too light. It wasn't how it should be. Nothing was. Not anymore. I had always liked rain, a fairly useful trait given how much it happened here. However, this wasn't real rain, not good, proper rain. It wasn't the sort of rain that beats down, heavily. The sort of rain that covers every-thing. The comforting, all-consuming sort of rain, that leaves nothing untouched. No. This was the pathetic kind of rain. With light, small raindrops that were barely visible. It was the kind of rain that was only noticeable because of the light mist it left on your jacket, and the pale, empty rain clouds it left in the sky. It might as well not bother.

I still remember everything about that day. I don't want to. I was sitting under the window when they told us. Hiding in the darkness. Crouched on the floor, holding my knees to my chest. I wanted to leave. Run. Hide. But I couldn't. They talked... explained... justified... I cried. I hated it. I remember the wind, drowning my words and blowing the pathetic rain around me. We walked on the beach that we'd been to a hundred times. I remem-ber asking questions I'd never cared about. Sandworms. Birds. Random Facts. I wanted to be talked to. I wanted to understand...

The beach was loud. Louder than my head. The waves crashed onto the shore. Pulsing, and lapping, and dragging themselves back out to sea. Fast. Angry. Dark. The waves were shouting, yelling, screaming just like I was inside. I didn't know what to think. Everything was changing. Everything was different.

The tide was far enough out. We walked along the beach to the waterfall. Where the heavy water was crashing, plummeting, falling down onto the rocks. Down. Down. Down. Plummeting towards us. Closer, and closer, and closer. Falling and following down a journey well known. This hadn't changed. This wouldn't change. Never. They couldn't change this. For this I was glad.

The beach was quiet, empty, deserted. It felt right. Calming. No one wants to be at the beach on a cold summer's day, standing in the pathetic rain. But I was. We were, and I am so glad.

Everything is different now. Everything is dark. Everything but the sky…

It wouldn't be dark for ages. It never would be. I always liked that. How it was never dark in summer. Long, never-ending days. Where the sun didn't set until after ten and rose long before anyone was up. That was both my favourite thing, and the only thing I didn't like. I liked the sunrise. It wasn't as good in summer when the sun would rise at 4am to an already blue sky. Dull. It *needed* darkness. Depended on it. Relied on it.

Nothing was the same after that day. Even time moved differently. Things happened slowly and quickly, and all at once. I spent a lot of time outside. Running. I didn't know where else to be. Nothing felt normal. Nothing felt right. Nothing used to be dark. Not outside anyway…

That changed.

Sunrise was better in winter – the darkness made it better. Maybe that was because you could see the darkness changing. Leaving. Ending. A new beginning. Watching the sky change from black to orange to blue. Winter. A gradual change, that happened all too quickly. And suddenly the sky glowed. Burnt orange. Yellow. Pink. A blazing fire encompassed everything around you. Destroying the darkness that had come before it. The flaming horizon floated above the sea. Hot and cold. Whilst smoke travelled up from your mouth flying into the fire. Flying home. The sun glared, glinted, gleamed as the frost glittered on the ground. The air was sharp and cold and clean. New. Untouchable. Nothing would destroy this.

I remember the rain; it rained a lot that winter. I liked that. It was helpful. Heavy. Dark. Cleansing. The darkness lasted forever. The days and the months merged together. I was broken. Grasping on to anything. Nothing worked. Everything was dark now. Everything...

I didn't know what to do...

Why?

I didn't know.

Looking back, it was obvious. I should have seen it, but I guess I didn't know what to look for. Or maybe I just didn't want to see it. I hadn't noticed anything. Nothing. How hadn't I noticed?

It was a dark winter...

Summer was long gone.

AIMEE GUTHREE

## The road south

The A961 runs all the way from Burwick, on the south-west of the island of South Ronaldsay, to the junction at the gates of the Bignold Park on the outskirts of Kirkwall. The road crosses the four 'Churchill' barriers built by Italian prisoners of WWII, designed to block Nazi German U-boats from entering Scapa Flow, where the Naval fleet of Britain lay. As you cross the barriers, you can see the remnants of blockships, especially during low tides, oxidised monoliths serving as a reminder of times less peaceful.

But the history, and the views, are not what makes this road special for me.

Once you have crossed the first barrier (or last chronologically on this journey) from Lamb's Holm to the mainland and have passed Holm village, there is nothing left of the long slog up the A9. The road at this point is long and straight, the sky deep and blue in the early evening and eventually, you reach a steep hill. As you climb it, you begin to realise where you are and at the top, you know that you are home.

The road comes to a corner at the hill's apex, and from here a brilliant view of Kirkwall unfolds. From Scapa beach to Hatston pier, Wideford hill to the Highland Park, the low sun casting tall shadows across the town centre. From here, the town can look so small, in comparison the cities you've just been in seem colossal. But here is where the primary school that you went to when you were 'peedie' is, where the shop where you had your first weekend job is, where the cathedral and the peedie sea and the palaces are, and perhaps most importantly, where your 'own bed' is.

Perhaps their holiday coming to an end has depressed them, with the thought that it may well be another year until they leave the islands again, or relieved that any car journeys for the foreseeable future won't exceed half an hour, but every Orcadian, upon first conversation with a relative or friend after returning from a trip 'sooth', has invariably spoken the phrase, 'Well, it's fine to be back in my own bed.' And, to be fair, after two weeks of hotel mattresses, your own bed can feel rather luxurious.

LEE TAYLOR

Finally, many thanks to head teacher Don Hawkins for supporting the project and English teacher Heather Spence for her work with the students in getting the writing done.

CHAPTER FORTY-EIGHT

# The Last Straw?

Fair Isle sweater.

WORKING WITH NATURAL materials, such as straw, grass, heather and hair, to make everyday items for the home or farm or croft, once widespread and an everyday activity, is largely a thing of the past in Orkney. The use of oat straw for the backs of Orkney chairs continues to thrive, however, with several established makers doing a good trade. Orkney chairs are highly valued items of furniture in many Orkney homes and in those of Orcadians around the world. Visitors, having fallen in love with these islands, often order one for their own home to remind them of Orkney when they're away south. My Orkney chair was a retirement gift to myself in 2006 when I lived in Derbyshire. Now it's come home and resides in my porch in Orphir Village.

Orkney chairs are not made out of necessity anymore. The style arose when it was discovered chairs could be made from straw which was much more readily available in Orkney than wood. Any wood the crofter had would have been needed for other jobs. Early Orkney chairs were limited to just four short wooden feet. Later on, a compromise was reached as a chair could be made more quickly by nailing together four wooden sides to form the base (a drawer could also be included) with just a straw back. Imagine the thrill when the man of the house had his own drawer for his whisky, pipe, tobacco and Bible. The woman may have kept knitting accoutrements in her drawer which, incidentally, was often to the side so it could be opened without her full skirt getting in the way. Woe betide anyone found trespassing in the other's drawer – or worse, being guilty of 'tidying it up'.

Island stories circulate readily in Orkney and I've already heard the same ones several times in different quarters having been here only two years. Here are a few versions of Orkney chair lore:

> The woman's chair had a hood to protect her from the draught at the croft house door.

> It was the man's chair that had the hood, to protect him from the draught, and the clamour of the children as he dozed by the fire.

> The woman's chair had no hood so she could see around to keep an eye on the children and the door for when visitors arrived.

> People just made whatever they fancied and had the time and materials for.

This last opinion was offered by Robert Towers, who made my chair for me, and was echoed by folk at the Dounby Straw Evening Class I visited back in October. It has the ring of truth.

David Kirkness (1854–1936) was a Kirkwall maker of straw-backed chairs, starting up his own business in the 1880s. He made the wooden framework and straw seats but bought in the straw backs from skilled makers in Westray, Papay and Deerness. During his lifetime he made over 14,000 chairs which went all over the world with some now in royal households.

Orkney chairs continue to be made as luxury items. They are cultural icons and, whilst they may not be the most comfortable for modern living, they complete any Orcadian room and provide a beautiful talking point for visitors – who go away with whichever version of the truth you choose to give them. Almost all the other uses for straw have slipped into the pages of history. Roofs, horse tack, baskets, bags, ropes and even boots are now more easily bought from specialist manufacturers and do the job a lot better.

There was a time, at the beginning of the 19th century, when straw working became a substantial industry for Orcadian girls and women making straw hats. By 1841, around 2,000 women worked in the industry – Orkney's first such. At one stage, they worked communally in the town but the 'factory' became a magnet for young men leading to concerns about morality. The work was dispersed to the outlying communities where there was more opportunity for chaperoning. The girls still got together in each other's homes with opportunity for chat while they worked. Fashions come and go, however, and by the 1870s significant straw plaiting in Orkney had come to an end.

In 1874, Hannah Primrose, Countess of Rosebery and Midlothian, inherited her father's fortune to become the richest woman in Britain. Lady Rosebery set up the Scottish Home Industries Association (SHIA) in 1889. (She died the following year aged just 39.) The aim of the SHIA was to support and encourage crofting industries in Scotland, particularly in the Highlands and Islands, and help them get a market and a fair price for their goods. It led directly to the Harris Tweed Association and the Crofters' Agency. Had the Association appeared 20 years earlier, it might have been in time to give some support and new direction to the straw plaiting girls in Orkney.

Once upon a time, almost everything the Orkney crofter had was homemade. Money was scarce and, even had it been plentiful, most things could not be bought. The men and women turned to what was available on the land and fabricated everything they needed from it. Straw was the mainstay – literally. They twisted rope (sookans) from oat straw and stronger rope (simmans) which had two strands twisted together. The simmans thatched the roof and held down the stacks. If time or straw was in short supply then sookans had to do. There are very few left who can make a good quality simmans. Simmans and sookans were rolled into balls called clews until needed. When a man could lay on a ball and only just touch the ground at each side then a clew was big enough. Any bigger and it probably wouldn't roll into the barn. Heather was used in extremis but, being stiff and coarse, it fell out of use when straw became more plentiful.

Horse collars (wazzies) and their back coverings (flaikies) were straw. Sacks and baskets of every conceivable size shape and application (cubbies and caisies) were made by men and women. Besom brushes were made of straw and even boots (strae beuts – more like leggings than boots). A length of sookan would be wound under the foot then round and round the leg to be tucked in at the top below the knee. They were fine on icy mornings but probably didn't last beyond lunch time. Women almost never wore strae beuts save one who favoured them. She came in for some ridicule (yes, even in the 19th century) and her penchant for strae beuts was explained on account of her being 'an isles body' (from the outer isles). Beds were universally of straw and used by rich and poor alike.

Eventually stone flags started to be used on roofs and a layer of straw about a foot thick would be laid on top to seal all the cracks. This would be secured by simmans in the usual way, stones being looped into the simmans at the eaves to hold them down. Prior to the use of flags, the roof would be straw and simmans alone – which was less than perfect as a roof covering. Put simply, they leaked in heavy rain. The layer of soot from the fire that had accumulated on the under surface would run down the inside wall in a slow, black trickle. It may even drip straight down into someone's porridge or down the back of a neck. In the worst storms, one had to retire to the box bed for shelter and, even then, containers were needed on the roof of it to catch drips. I have heard it said that warmth and comfort were not given such high priorities in the 1800s. I find that surprising.

In October 2019, I visited Elsie Wishart and the straw working group in Dounby. They operate as a night class in the Masonic Hall, just behind the Co-op. It was dark by 7.30pm, nights were clearly drawing in and the time of year had come again for such pastimes.

I found Elsie and the ladies (they were mostly ladies) hard at work on a range of items – Orkney chairs, caisies and cubbies mostly. Strae beuts did not seem to be in evidence and it didn't look as if anyone was preparing to reroof a croft house with simmans. That said, one could been forgiven for thinking straw skills are alive and flourishing in Orkney. There was a working atmosphere in the room (of about a dozen people). The happy chatter subsided when I got my camera out. Heads dipped a bit but soon rose again and I was able to snap some smiling faces.

Elsie has been running the group since 1982. She doesn't like the idea of being called the boss.

> I take the tea, biscuits, cheese and oatcakes for the supper. That usually starts at 9.00pm and goes on till 9.30pm, or maybe 10.00pm, depending on how much yarn and chatter there is. The council used to run it, with a proper teacher – Willie Stevenson – but he retired and I took it on with Sheila Wylie, but she has since retired too. I learned everything from Willie. I had not done straw work or even seen it done before I started here. There was quite a strong tradition of straw work in Westray at one time and we used to get chair frames from there to finish. It was difficult to get frames made here. We aren't a commercial operation. People just come and make things for themselves and their friends and families. The social aspect is very important. We have nights out before we start each autumn, then one at Christmas and another when we finish. We always have a Burns supper here – we bring haggis and all the trimmings. I don't know who would take

over if I retired. When I broke my ankle a few years ago, they cancelled the sessions till I got better. I guess somebody would come forward. Everyone agrees it would be awful if straw working died out in Orkney so someone would do it. They wanted me to go down to South Ronaldsay one evening a week to help with a group there but I don't fancy the barriers in the winter. I wouldn't mind if a carload from there came here though – they'd be very welcome.

Orkney chair-making seems secure. Makers can charge a good price for their time, skill and materials, they can make a living from it. Baskets and cradles, however, do not command prices to reflect the time taken to make them. Everyone wants one. Visitors and locals alike love to have a piece of straw work with the 'traditionally handmade in Orkney' label but for how much longer will such things be available?

A few years ago, Catherine Lock travelled all the way from her shop – The New Craftsmen – in Mayfair to work with Kevin Gauld – The Orkney Furniture Maker – on the development of new ideas and new markets for Orkney furniture. The collaboration was successful and, in 2019, Catherine was back with other craft workers to explore the place of straw working and heather working in Orkney at the beginning of the 21st century. It will come as no surprise that Catherine concluded that the skills are hanging by a thread. Unless new people can be recruited and taught then when the present generation of weavers becomes the past generation, the skills will be lost forever. They will not be relearned from books or videos. Catherine would like to explore the idea of a straw school in Orkney where small numbers of people come, for a few days initially, to learn the craft from skilled people. The format could be similar to the way in which people enjoy painting, photographic or pottery holidays.

We've lost skills before – stone axe-making, preparing hides by hand for example, and we still don't know how the stone circles were built, but are we any worse off? Would it matter if someone in the Dounby group was the one to make the last basket in Orkney? I think it would.

All may not be lost. Shortly after I finished this chapter, I met Jackie and Marlene Miller at Scapa Crafts in Kirkwall. They have been making Orkney chairs at their home on the edge of town for almost 30 years. I visited them in their workshop and we sat, in Orkney chairs, surrounded by more Orkney chairs in various stages of completion and an assortment of expressions – with hoods, without hoods, with or without draws and easy fit (ostensibly to give more room for knitting elbows but good for the fuller figure too). There was oat straw piled in the corner and historic pictures of chairs gone by on the walls. As true exponents of the local craft, Jackie and Marlene were invited to exhibit at the Smithsonian Institute in Washington DC in 2002. They spent two weeks working flat out at an international craft fair there.

What may yet turn out to be Jackie and Marlene's lasting legacy, however, is the time and patience put into teaching the next generation of chair makers – and the one after that. Daughter Bridget is a fair hand at it, as are her children Leah (19) and Magnus (16). Daughter Caroline's two – Harvey (18) and Owen (20) – are also trained. There is always a risk of Orkney's youngsters being lost to the bright lights in the south, but I wouldn't bet against at least one member of the family taking over when university is done and when the time comes.

## CHAPTER FORTY-NINE
# Energy

AUTHOR'S PROMISE TO you, dear reader: science content of this chapter will not exceed GCSE level. It's stuff you need to know anyway.

Watt (w) = unit of power or energy use.

Kilowatt (KW) = 1,000 watts (think: one bar electric fire).

Megawatt (MW) = 1,000,000 watts (Eurostar loco uses 12MW).

Gigawatt (GW) = 1,000,000,000 watts (2 per cent UK total energy need)

If James Watt had foreseen the unlooked-for side effects of the industrial revolution would he have pressed ahead with development of the steam engine? If they had known at the time how polluted the world would become would they have cared? The pollution and climate change we are facing at present is largely due to the exploitation of fossil fuels (coal and oil) to power Watt's steam engines and their successors. Don't get me wrong, I'm not blaming James Watt for any of this.

The search is on for ever more energy efficient ways of doing things and for ways of supplying that energy in a way that does not induce climate change. Energy efficiency is found by streamlining vehicles and making them lighter. It is found by insulating houses, fitting LED light bulbs and a whole bunch of other measures. Climate friendly energy generation is basically any method that does not involve burning coal, oil or gas – the so-called fossil fuels.

Let me take a moment to run through the basic science for those readers who may not have got to grips with this whole idea yet. Please be aware this is a simple summary of a few key points. Other interpretations are available. You can skip the next four, italicised paragraphs if you're already happy with the concepts.

*Green plants, especially trees because they're big and there's a lot of them, absorb carbon dioxide gas from the atmosphere. Animals breathe out carbon dioxide gas. They have been doing this quite happily for millions of years. For most of history, the amount of carbon dioxide in the air never changed much because the trees and the animals balanced each other out. During the Carboniferous Period, around 300 million years ago, the Earth was covered by large swamp forests. When trees died and became compressed by other trees growing on top, they fossilised into coal. Coal is a fossil tree – hence 'fossil fuels'. Most of the carbon the tree had absorbed during its life was trapped in the coal.*

*There it lay, for millions of years, until people discovered they could burn it and make heat. Coal miners began digging it up in vast quantities and burning it to produce heat and electricity for all manner of things – the Industrial Revolution. The carbon locked up in the coal, which had taken millions of years to collect by the forests, was suddenly all being released into the air (in the form of carbon dioxide gas) in a matter of a couple of hundred years. Modern trees can't absorb it quickly enough so it is now accumulating in the air.*

*The carbon dioxide gas acts like a sheet of glass around the Earth (like the ceiling of a greenhouse) so heat from the sun reaches the Earth through the atmosphere but can't escape (just like in a greenhouse on a sunny day). The Earth and oceans and atmosphere heat up (causing global warming) and carbon dioxide becomes known as a greenhouse gas.*

*As a result of global warming, deserts start spreading and encroaching on agricultural land; ice melts, causing sea levels to rise and coastal communities to be threatened; oceans heat up causing fish to seek cooler parts; weather becomes more extreme, causing floods and other natural disasters. It's all quite worrying really, so I'll get back to the search for climate-friendly energy generators. One last thought before I do that, however: President Trump thinks it's all a hoax – fake news. There is no global warming. What if he's right? What if all the tree huggers and cyclists are simply wasting their time? Could be, but do you want to wait to find out after it's too late? Or do you think we should do something about it just in case? At the very least we could save money and make the coal last longer.*

In 1980, on holiday in France, I stayed in a *gite* with a black rubber hose pipe coiled up on the roof and connected to the mains water supply at one end and the shower at the other. During the day, it heated up in the sun and every evening we got a hot shower out of it. It was my first experience of green energy. The hose was basically an early solar panel. It seemed like a French novelty that would never be any good in the UK because it isn't sunny enough. Now solar panels are everywhere, efficient and cost effective. In 1988, during my first visit to Orkney, I saw one of the first experimental wind turbines to supply electricity to the National Grid. Now the technology is proven and they are all around us. The moral of these anecdotes is to have faith and keep working. We are already at a point where electricity generated from green sources is a measurable percentage of energy requirements. Who'd have believed that possible when looking at the black hose pipe on the *gite* roof in 1980?

Orkney has a seemingly limitless supply of wind so is a good place to put wind turbines – if you like wind turbines that is. It also has incredibly powerful waves and tides which is why it has become the world capital for the development of generators that can extract energy from waves and tides. At a very rough estimate the theoretical maximum total energy in Orkney, from wind, waves and tides, is about 5 gigawatts (5GW). That's about enough for 3,500,000 homes, or about 10 per cent of the UK's energy need.

Some years ago, before we all got excited about renewables. (Incidentally, perhaps this is another term I should explain. Wind, wave and tidal energy are called renewable energy sources because there is an inexhaustible supply of them – they are constantly being renewed. Compare this with coal of which there is a fixed and limited supply. No new coal will be made after all the mines are empty.) Two cables were laid between Orkney and the Scottish mainland, each one capable of carrying 30 megawatts of electricity. They were there to supply Orkney with mains electricity generated further south. There was a 30MW supply cable plus a spare – total capacity 60MW. Jump forwards a few decades and Orkney is generating all the electricity it needs from renewables and is able to export 60MW back down the cables to Scotland. The cables are therefore full.

Orkney is the world capital for research and development of wave and tidal energy generation. Yes, tiny Orkney, population around 22,000, and out here on the edge of the known universe is that capital. There are more wave and tidal generating devices in the water at any one time than in any other single location. The European Marine Energy Centre (EMEC) is here and we have all the skills, facilities, resources, staff, waves and tides you could possibly wish for to test your devices. Unfortunately, until recently, there was nothing we could do with the electricity you might generate. Orkney couldn't use it and the cables for export were already full. Development companies, in the later stages of testing their devices, want to be able to run them at full output for six months to prove them. In extreme cases, wind turbines were being turned off to allow marine generators access to some grid capacity. What to do?

The obvious plan is to get more cable capacity and that is certainly an option being seriously looked at. It will cost about £200 million to install a 200 MW cable. Neil Kermode, the director of EMEC, told me that is the sort of cheque that governments sign every day. It sounds a lot but compared with, say, the total spent on yoghurt in a year or cleaning wet wipes out of our water pipes (£100 million by the way) then it's not too bad. A 'needs case' has to be made to Ofgen to justify the new cable. Ofgen is insisting that a sufficient number of electricity suppliers sign up to use the cable should it be installed, in order to justify the expense of it. In February 2019, suppliers had pledged to supply at least 80 MW but Ofgen are asking for a 135 MW commitment.

'Be careful what you wish for,' someone once said. A new cable might simply open the flood gates to installers of wind turbines beating a path to Orkney and asking to put up more, taller, bigger turbines. The technology is proven and planners might be tempted by a quick fix to supplying the new cable with electricity. If Orkney doesn't provide the conditions for marine (wave and tide) companies, they will simply go elsewhere in the world. Neil Kermode thinks there is room for compromise – maybe something like 135 MW of wind generation and 65 MW of marine input.

Orkney is a fabulous place for tidal experiments. It is estimated that 4 giga watts of tidal energy pass through the Pentland Firth at peak flow. This is a terrible current for mariners – it has claimed lives, wrecked ships and I even heard of a cruise liner being laid over at 45 degrees when it got into a tidal eddy. Incredibly, no one was injured but much food and crockery was spoiled (the passengers were at dinner) and officers on the bridge had to cling on to anything that was screwed down until the ship righted herself. This was all because the autopilot had been left on. The bow of the ship nosed into a powerful eddy and was pushed one way whilst the stern was still trying to go the other. Something had to give so the ship did the only thing it could do in the circumstances and leaned over.

I often ponder what conditions must be like in the Firth, usually on a dark, stormy Thursday night when I'm sitting listening to the Strathspey and Reel Society in the winter. The music always reminds me of where I am, which is why thoughts turn to the sea. In my head, I have imagined installing enough tidal generators across the Pentland Firth to capture all the 4 GW of power. Of course, this would close the lane to shipping and, interestingly, if I installed just one unit too many would completely stop the flow and then we should get nothing. The water, then, would have to find another way round between North Sea and Atlantic so look out anyone trying to sail a boat north of Stroma or in Scapa Flow.

A look at the map of Orkney shows the islands of Westray (lying NW/SE) and Sanday (lying NE/SW) forming a huge tidal funnel, with Eday (N/S) almost filling the narrow neck of the funnel. EMEC have installed a tidal test site in the Falls of Warness off the SW tip of Eday. The strong tides here pouring out of the funnel make it ideal. Neil Kermode told me that installing just a single turbine on the SE side of Eday is enough to disrupt the flow round the island so that, not only is energy extracted on the SW side, but also a tiny bit extra is got from Falls of Warness on the west. Who'd have thought it?

Industry brains are already looking beyond the drive to produce and export ever more electricity from Orkney. We do not, after all, want to turn the islands into nothing more than an offshore power station for the Scottish Central Belt. Creative thinkers have already set up machinery to extract hydrogen gas from seawater. (Every molecule of water contains two atoms of hydrogen and one of oxygen. It can quite easily be split by electrolysis into the two constituent gases, using electricity from renewable sources.) Currently the hydrogen is being stored in tanks then used to run fuel cells which can power cars, buses and ferries.

Beyond pure hydrogen, there could be synthetically produced ammonia (from hydrogen and nitrogen) which has 40 per cent the calorific value of diesel. Further, carbon could be extracted from carbon dioxide and incorporated with hydrogen and nitrogen to make synthetic hydrocarbon fuels. I can hear some readers screaming at this point that hydrocarbon fuels are what caused the problem in the first place, but here is the simple, fantastic, genius beauty of the plan: these are not fossil hydrocarbons but newly created ones. We would be extracting carbon from the atmosphere on Monday, burning fuel and re-releasing the carbon on Tuesday, then re-capturing the carbon to make more fuel on Wednesday. The average carbon content of the atmosphere would not change as a result of this process. In the end it's not burning hydrocarbon fuel that's the problem, provided it comes from a renewable source. (There is still the problem to be tackled of air pollution near homes causing asthma and other respiratory illnesses.)

In a final, for now, elegant twist to the Orkney Green Energy story, the Flotta Oil Terminal sits just six miles across Scapa Flow from where I am sitting. When the oil from the Piper Bravo field in the North Sea is exhausted and Flotta becomes redundant, instead of pulling it down we could apply to the Orkney Islands Council for a change of use order. Flotta could be the world's first green hydrocarbon fuel plant.

## CHAPTER FIFTY

# The Green Red Boat

ANDREW BANKS OBE is an Orcadian entrepreneur. In 2001, he began a ferry service on the short-sea crossing from Gills Bay in Caithness, three miles west of John O' Groats, to St Margaret's Hope in South Ronaldsay, Orkney. He started with ex-Caledonian MacBrayne boats: *Iona* (renamed *Pentalina-b*) followed by MV *Claymore*, before his own catamaran, purpose-built in the Philippines – MV *Pentalina*. *Pentalina* has now been superseded by another catamaran – MV *Alfred* – which came into service on 1 November 2019, having been built in Vietnam.

Alfred was named after Andrew's late father who sadly passed away a few months before the ship came home to Orkney. I was lucky enough to have a ticket for the inaugural crossing and, together with fellow passengers, mostly carrying cameras, declared the ship to be very well appointed. The crossing takes only an hour so the comfy seat by the window, clean toilets, serving hatch for coffee and a snack meant the ship had everything I needed. Add to those the children's play area and dog-friendly lounge and everyone was happy.

The really exciting aspect of the service for me, however, is the environmental impact (or lack of impact) of the ship. *Alfred* is a catamaran so has no need to carry 100 tons of ballast as an equivalent mono-hull must do. Ballast is dead weight, fuel is required to carry it back and forth, endlessly, without generating any revenue and yet still emitting pollutants.

The hulls themselves have a combined width much less than a mono-hull and therefore can be pushed through the water for the expenditure of significantly less fuel. Andrew told me that, per car carried per mile, the *Alfred* is around ten times more fuel efficient than a comparable mono-hulled ship.

The bit I really liked was the ability of the ship to be plugged into the mains power on the pier each night when she ties up. There are two 14-man crews living on board in a two-week rotation so all their heating, lighting and cooking comes through the shore connection (like a caravan) instead of with the cost, noise and air pollution that would result from running the ship's generators all night. Quieter for the crew and anyone living close by the pier. As if that wasn't enough, the power comes from wind turbines owned by the company. When the wind blows, as it often does in Orkney, the power is free and clean but can be topped up from the grid on calm days. The offices, stores and workshops on the pier are similarly supplied.

When I met Andrew at his office to talk about his new venture, he was wearing a hi-vis jacket that wasn't easy to see because of all the grime on the front from wiping his similarly grimy hands. His jeans had seen better days too.

'I thought you would have been a suit and tie man,' I told him.

'Someone has to do the work,' he said.

Andrew is a family man and Pentland Ferries is a family business in which he is supported by wife Susan plus daughters Kathryn, Laura and Jenni and son David. He did clean up and put on a suit (kilt actually) for his day at Buckingham Palace in 2014 when Her Majesty the Queen awarded him an OBE for the work he has done in providing this ferry service to Orkney.

Pentland Ferries receives no government money and yet has proved a fast, reliable ferry service that can operate in almost all weathers across the Pentland Firth, one of the most turbulent 15 miles of water in the world. When push comes to shove and when climate change problems force world governments so far into the corner that they absolutely have to make travel as efficient as possible, short of banning it altogether, then catamarans and wind turbines may well be part of the solution. If Andrew Banks says 'I told you so' then who would blame him.

CHAPTER FIFTY-ONE

# Orkney Life and the Power to Heal

IT'S ORKNEY, NEVER The Orkneys. *Orc* may derive from Pictish for pig or boar. In the late 9th century, Norwegian settlers interpreted the name as deriving from *orkn* (seal). They made the name *Orkneyjar* meaning seal islands. *Jar* (meaning islands) was eventually dropped, since *ey* alone conveys the idea of island or islands. There are 74, of which 20 are inhabited.

It's often windy in winter. One day at the end of November, the ferry from Scrabster blew down the narrow harbour of Stromness sideways in a southerly gale, doing about 5 knots. Shoppers, dog-walkers and bus drivers stopped to see what would happen. A few yards from the pier the boat's powerful bow thrusters turned her head windward and she slid backwards onto the berth without so much as a bump. The skipper's done that before we all agreed. The bus to St Margaret's Hope had to wait for passengers (many of them green) from the ferry.

Work, too, is occasionally disrupted by the weather. If one has to visit the south isles from Kirkwall for instance, and a gale coincides with high tide, it may have to be postponed if waves are breaking over the causeways. A few years ago, the emergency doctor's car was trapped and she was rescued by a 24-year-old policewoman who received a medal for her effort.

Said ferry (MV *Hamnavoe*) has to go for her annual refit each January and, usually, folk are up in arms about her planned replacement. MV *Helliar* is a cargo vessel with only 12 passenger spaces and no adequate disabled facilities. It's only for a week and there are other routes off the island so maybe it's just a storm in a teacup. In 2020, there has been some suggestion the redundant

*Pentalina* could act as stand-in, now the new *Alfred* has come onto the Gill's Bay to St Margaret's Hope run.

We get most of the new release films at the cinema in the leisure centre. We've enjoyed a lot of the popular releases but they don't stay very long so one has to be prepared for 11.ooam or 2.oopm showings to fit them in. I got my ticket for a performance of Rutter's *Magnificat* performed by the Orkney Winter Choir (with Bev as a soprano) and *Orkney Camerata* in St Magnus Cathedral in mid-December. Tickets for the fabulous Wrigley Sisters' (Jenny on fiddle and Hazel on guitar) Hogmanay concert are always hot items. I snap ours up early to avoid disappointment. 8.oopm to 10.oopm, back home for bed before midnight, in time to miss all the nonsense on the telly.

The winter visitors are here as I sit in my room writing this. Forty thousand greylag geese in the fields and whooper swans on the lochs. Wigeon, goldeneye and long-tailed duck are on the lochs too, and even on the town pond (known as the Peedie (Little) Sea). Redwing, fieldfare, snow buntings and bramblings have all blown through on their way south. Fulmars are already prospecting for nest sites on the cliffs below the house. Walking down the path to the cliff the other day I could hear eider ducks calling from quite a way off.

Harvest Home in the village school is a calendar fixture in November. I was put on tattie peeling so made sure I had my sharp peeler with me. We had clapshot[1] and cold meats last year with clootie dumpling and coffee to follow. Everyone helped to serve and clear away. A couple of times I walked into the hall with two bowls of pudding but there was no one to serve, because they were all serving. Tables cleared it was time for stripping the willow.

Thursday morning means time to wander up to the kirk for coffee and home bakes. Eleanor is my self-appointed dialect coach

---

[1] Clapshot is an Orcadian dish prepared by mashing tatties (potatoes) and neeps (turnips) together with onions and a few chives if you're feeling posh. Clootie dumpling is spotted dick basically.

and greets me with such utterances as, 'Noo, rattle that doon yer thrapple and fill yer puggy.'

I usually sit with Maria (92), an incomer, like me, having survived the war in Germany she arrived in 1947 from Austria, and Johnny (95) – a native Orcadian famous for beachcombing and with a shed full of bits of WWII battleships. The post office sets up in the vestry in the afternoon so one can buy stamps and pay bills at the same time. Otherwise it's a seven-mile trip into the toon (Kirkwall) for the main office.

Orkney Island Council has just spent £200,000 on three deserted islands: Faray (300 acres), Holm of Faray (80 acres) and Red Holm (5 acres). They have been uninhabited since 1947. £519 per acre would seem very reasonable (building plots in Kirkwall can be as high as £100,000 – if you can get one.) Faray, however, has no electricity, running water, sewage, roads, ferry, air service or nurse. Fine if you fancy living off-grid. There is talk of a wind farm being developed there which would mean less intrusion for the populated islands. The folk on neighbouring Eday and Westray might be less pleased about their views being spoiled.

Had we lived in our house 100 years ago we would have seen, from our kitchen window, the entire German High Seas Fleet described in Chapter 30. We had a two-day conference recently. Grandchildren of British, American and German naval worthies led the discussions.

Never a dull moment. Just six hours of daylight in December but come Christmas we are racing round the sun to glorious June when it hardly sets.

\* \* \*

I'd not had a good week. You might say I'd had a very bad week – the worst, in fact, of the 65 weeks I'd lived in Orkney up to that point. By comparison to other global, national and personal problems, it was nothing really. One of my projects had suffered a setback but I was feeling rather sorry for myself.

I went to the Service of Nine Lessons and Carols at St Magnus Cathedral on the Sunday night, shortly before Christmas, and came out feeling much better. It wasn't an epiphany, I don't consider myself religious, I just enjoyed the music.

There is a bit more to it than that. There were all the familiar carols of childhood – the same tunes, rhythm and tempo. The same words. Carols are where I learned the meaning of words such as 'abhor' (as in: 'Lo, he abhors not the virgin's womb'); also 'lo', 'virgin' and 'womb' come to that. Throw in 'lowly', 'manger', 'meek' and 'reconciled' and you have the germ of a Christmas lexicon.

I was comforted. Although I now consider Orkney my home and I am very happy here, at times of self-doubt I miss my mum and dad and here was an occasion very like the ones I shared with them 60 years ago. Here were all the elements of a childhood Christmas: carols, candles, the tree, peace and wonder at a timeless story of love.

I always look up into the arches and vaults in St Magnus and wonder at the incredible achievement and motivation required

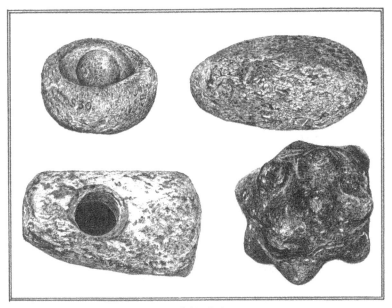

Neolithic finds.

to build it here, on this tiny island anchored in the fierce rip of the Pentland Firth. As I sat listening to the choir, there was, out in the blackness of the night, around Stroma and Muckle Skerry and Swona, the most terrible swirling water, trying to dislodge the land and carry it off, either into the Atlantic or the North Sea.

In my island-hopping days, to places such as Staffa, Mingulay and St Kilda, I relished a few basic luxuries – food, shelter, fire and a good book – to separate me from the harsher realities of my temporary home. Here, in the cathedral, however, island life had reached a much higher plane. There was warmth and smiles and song and a few exchanged greetings with neighbours, companion-ship and blessing.

# **Luath** Press Limited

*committed to publishing well written books worth reading*

LUATH PRESS takes its name from Robert Burns, whose little collie Luath (*Gael.*, swift or nimble) tripped up Jean Armour at a wedding and gave him the chance to speak to the woman who was to be his wife and the abiding love of his life. Burns called one of the 'Twa Dogs' Luath after Cuchullin's hunting dog in Ossian's *Fingal*.
Luath Press was established in 1981 in the heart of Burns country, and is now based a few steps up the road from Burns' first lodgings on Edinburgh's Royal Mile. Luath offers you distinctive writing with a hint of unexpected pleasures.
Most bookshops in the UK, the US, Canada, Australia, New Zealand and parts of Europe, either carry our books in stock or can order them for you. To order direct from us, please send a £sterling cheque, postal order, international money order or your credit card details (number, address of cardholder and expiry date) to us at the address below. Please add post and packing as follows: UK – £1.00 per delivery address; overseas surface mail – £2.50 per delivery address; overseas airmail – £3.50 for the first book to each delivery address, plus £1.00 for each additional book by airmail to the same address. If your order is a gift, we will happily enclose your card or message at no extra charge.

## **Luath** Press Limited
543/2 Castlehill
The Royal Mile
Edinburgh EH1 2ND
Scotland
Telephone: +44 (0)131 225 4326 (24 hours)
email: sales@luath. co.uk
Website: www. luath.co.uk